Bibliographic information published by the German National Library:

The German National Library lists this publication in the National Bibliography; detailed bibliographic data are available on the Internet at http://dnb.dnb.de .

Imprint:

Copyright © 2016 GRIN Verlag
Print and binding: Books on Demand GmbH, Norderstedt Germany
ISBN: 9783668951891

This book at GRIN:

https://www.grin.com/document/470009

Thura Ali Khalaf

Design and Implementation of Iris Pattern Recognition Based on Wireless Network Systems

GRIN Verlag

GRIN - Your knowledge has value

Since its foundation in 1998, GRIN has specialized in publishing academic texts by students, college teachers and other academics as e-book and printed book. The website www.grin.com is an ideal platform for presenting term papers, final papers, scientific essays, dissertations and specialist books.

Visit us on the internet:

http://www.grin.com/

http://www.facebook.com/grincom

http://www.twitter.com/grin_com

Design and Implementation of Iris Pattern Recognition Based on Wireless Network System

A Thesis
Submitted to the College of Information Engineering
at Al-Nahrain University in Partial Fulfillment of the Requirements
for the Degree of Master of Science
in
Information and Communication Engineering

By
Thura Ali Khalaf
(B.Sc. in Internet Engineering 2013)

Dedicate

To the most beautiful and amazing woman on earth...
To the brightest candle of my life...
To my beloved mother (Hayfaa Alansari) ♡

With all my love...
Thura Ali

Abstract

The goal of this thesis is to propose a fast and accurate iris pattern recognition system based on wireless network system. This thesis presents three parts; in the first part, Libor Masek algorithm is enhanced to achieve higher recognition rate. Another method of iris pattern recognition is proposed which named genetic algorithm. The two used iris pattern recognition methods are compared according to their accuracy and execution time. When testing persons of the Chinese Academy of Sciences Institute of Automation (CASIA) database, both methods achieved 100% recognition rates because there is at least one image sample for each person, which is correct matched and there is no person that is false matched. But when testing image samples per persons of CASIA database, the genetic algorithm achieved higher recognition rates and lower error rates than Libor Masek algorithm. It has been found, that the recognition time of genetic algorithm is less than Masek algorithm.

The second part, presents an iris image compression/decompression by using Principal Component Analysis (PCA) for compression process and Inverse Principal Component Analysis (IPCA) for decompression process. It has been proven that PCA is the most suitable method for compressing iris images because of its ability to reduce their size while maintaining the good quality of the reconstructed images. Reconstructed images using IPCA have low compression ratios (CRs) and high Peak to Signal Ratios (PSNRs), which leads to good quality. For more security, a multi-stage image compression is performed in order to protect network's transmitted data from hackers because hackers cannot guess how much the image has been compressed.

I

The third part, includes wireless network system consisting of one central Personal Computer (PC) and four Personal Computers (PCs) that communicate with each other through router device. The central PC takes the responsibility of monitoring and controlling the PCs of the whole network. All network PCs communicate with each other by using Transmission Control Protocol /Internet Protocol (TCP/IP) protocol suite that use client-server sockets to transfer images between PCs on the network.

From the results obtained, both used iris pattern recognition methods were able to recognize reconstructed iris images. Genetic algorithm recognizes reconstructed iris image within less time than Masek algorithm. The first line takes less transmission time than the second line, because the first line is transmitting compressed iris images unlike the second line.

Table of Contents

List of Abbreviations

AP	Access Point
ATM	Asynchronous Transfer Mode
BMP	BitMaP
CASIA	Chinese Academy of Sciences' Institute of Automation
CCD	Charged Coupled Device
CR	Compression Ratio
CRR	Correct Recognition Rate
CI	Compression Index
dB	deciBel
DNA	DeoxyriboNucleic Acid
FAR	False Acceptance Rate
FRR	False Rejection Rate
HD	Hamming Distance
ICMP	Internet Control Message Protocol
IP	Internet Protocol
IPCA	Inverse Principal Component Analysis
IR	InfraRed
IER	Iris Effective Region
IEEE	Institute of Electrical and Electronics Engineers
LAN	Local Area Network
MAN	Metropolitan Area Network
MSE	Mean Square Error
NIR	Near-InfraRed
PCA	Principal Component Analysis

PC	Personal Computer
PIN	Personal Identification Number
PLS	Partial Least Squares
PSNR	Peak Signal to Noise Ratio
RMON	Remote Monitoring
RR	Recognition Rate
RGB	Red Green Blue
SNMP	Simple Network Monitoring Protocol
TCP	Transmission Control Protocol
VL	Visible Light
WiFi	Wireless Fidelity
WLAN	Wireless Local Area Network
WIMAX	Word wide Interoperability for Microwave Access

List of Symbols

Symbol	Meaning
$[A]$	Gray scale image matrix
a	Multi-scale 2D wavelet size parameter
a_j	Curvature
β	Multi-scale 2D wavelet size parameter
$CI(r,c)$	Centered image matrix
$CI(r,c)^T$	Transpose of the centered image matrix
f	Float number
F	Fitness of population
f_0	Center frequency
G_k	New generation
(h_i, k_i)	Peak of the parabola
$[I]$	Image matrix
$[I(r,c)]$	Image matrix
$[I_1(m,n)]$	Input image matrix
$[I_2(m,n)]$	Decompressed image matrix
Im	Imaginary part
$I(\rho, \phi)$	Iris image in polar coordinates
$I(x,y)$	Iris image
λ	Eigen value
$[MeanI]$	Mean image matrix
m	Size of vector
N	Total number of bits

N_{pr}	Number of problem dimensions
$Peakval$	Peak value
p	Problem
P_i	Probability of selection
Q_i	Cumulative probability
r	Radius of the circle
Re	Real part
(r, θ)	Normalized dimensionless polar coordinates
(r_0, θ_0)	Coordinates of the point for which the encoding process is applied
θ_j	Angle rotation
V	Eigen vector
v_i	Individual
w	Wavelet frequency
(x, y)	Original Cartesian coordinates
X, Y	Bit patters
(x_c, y_c)	Center coordinates
(x_i, y_i)	Coordinates of the iris
(x_p, y_p)	Coordinates of the pupil
σ	Bandwidth of the filter

List of Figures

XII

List of Tables

Chapter One
General Introduction

1.1 Introduction

Biometrics are methods of verifying a person based on a physiological characteristic. Examples of physiological characteristics include iris, face, fingerprint, and so on. Biometrics system uses hardware to capture the biometric features, and software to manipulate and manage the system. In general, the system converts these measurements into a mathematical, computer-readable format. When a user first creates a biometric profile, known as a template, that template is stored in the data storage or database. The biometrics system then compares this template to the new template created every time a user enters the system [1].

Iris pattern recognition security system is one of the most dependable prominent technologies for user verification. The human iris has random feature and it is stable throughout the life, it can serve as a living password or passport that can't be forgotten or lost [2].

The use of wireless technology is rapidly becoming the most popular way to connect a network. Wi-Fi technology is one of the several existing technologies that offer the convenience way of data transmitting without physical connection. In distributed biometric systems, the image acquisition stage is often dislocated from the feature extraction and matching stage. In such environments the image have to be transferred via a network link to the respective location, often over wireless channels with low bandwidth and high latency. Therefore, a minimization of the amount of data be transferred is highly desirable, which is achieved by compressing the data before transmission [3] [4].

1

1.2 Literature Survey

This work required research in three main fields, so the review is presented according to these fields, this review will focus on the researches in recent years as shown in Fig. 1-1.

In the iris pattern recognition field,

In 2009, Hosseini, et al. [5] used a shape analysis method to describe patterns and to derive feature-code for each subject. The investigation in the fusion of features extracted from Near-Infrared (NIR) and Visible Light (VL) imaging were proposed in order to boost the recognition performance. This investigation demonstrates that the proposed algorithm is highly sensitive to the patterns of cromophores and improves the iris recognition rate.

In 2010, Zhonghua and Bibo [6] presented an iris recognition method based on the coefficients of Morlet wavelet transform. Firstly, it locates the iris, then makes normalization to the iris image and gets 512columns multiplying 64 rows rectangular iris image. Secondly, it makes one dimension Morlet wavelet transform row by row to the iris image. Thirdly, it makes binary codes to the iris image. Finally, it sorts the different iris patterns by pattern matching method and gives the recognition results.

In 2011, Cho, et al. [7] presented a new algorithm for biometric-based iris recognition system. The proposed iris identification algorithm consists of four major fundamental steps: image processing; image localization; Iris Effective Region (IER) extraction; and image pattern recognition.

In 2012, Ramkumarl and Arumugam [8] proposed a new method of iris recognition, which localizes eye's pupil by using negative algorithm and four neighbors method.

Fig.1.1 Iris pattern recognition, Data reduction and Wireless network methods from 2007 to 2015.

And the iris boundary is detected by using contrast enhancement, special wedges. Thresholding techniques are used to separate the particular iris regions to be normalized later. The normalized iris is enhanced by using Histogram equalization technique. Cumulative sum based change analysis and hamming distance are used for feature extraction and matching process respectively.

In 2013, Mabrukar, et al. [9] detected the pupil-iris boundary by using circular Hough transform. They normalized the iris pattern for making computations easy by using Daugman's Rubber sheet model. Feature Extraction was done by using multiple scale Taylor series extension of the iris texture. Hough transform and Daugman's Rubber sheet model techniques were used in this research.

In 2014, Darabkh, et al. [10] introduced two new methods to implement feature extraction process. Both methods used a sliding-window technique and various mathematical operations on the pixels to make the feature vectors. Analysis of this two methods were done by preforming various performance measurements such as Recognition Rate (RR), False Acceptance Rate (FAR), and False Rejection Rate (FRR).

In 2015, Kashani, et al. [11] proposed an algorithm for the eye tracking by combining the pupil based Kalman filter with the mean shift algorithm. That used modal recognition technique and was based on the pictures with high equality of eye iris.

In the data reduction field,

In 2008, **Saikat Maitra and Jun Yan** [12] presented two methods, Principle Component Analysis (PCA) and Partial Least Squares (PLS), for dimension reduction in case that the distinct variables used in regression are extremely correlated.

4

In 2011, Sherin Kishk, et al. [13] proposed a technique that depend on applying PCA on the wavelet coefficients of the elemental pictures to progress the quality of the recovered 3 Dimensional (3D) image while attaining high compression ratio.

In 2012, Rafael do Espírito Santo [14] described the use of a statistical tool that called PCA for the recognition of patterns and compression. These concepts were applied to digital images used in Medicine.

In 2013, Karamizadeh, et al. [15] used PCA tool to compress multidimensional data to lower dimensions while keeping most of the information. It covers standard deviation, covariance, and eigenvectors.

In the wireless network field,

In 2007, Seifedine Kadry, and Khaled Smaili [16] designed a wireless iris recognition attendance system and the system is implemented by using Daugman's algorithm. This system based biometrics and wireless technique solves the problem of fake attendance and the problem of arranging the corresponding network.

1.3. Aim of the Work

The aim of this work is to design and implement an iris pattern recognition based on wireless network system.

The main steps can be summarized as follows:

- Develop and design a Graphical User Interface (GUI) of Libor Masek algorithm by using MATLAB program.
- Design and implement another method for iris pattern recognition by using genetic algorithm with the appropriate Graphical User Interface (GUI) by using MATLAB program.

- Make comparison between Libor Masek algorithm and the modified genetic algorithm based on performance and execution time.
- Design and Implement image compression algorithm to transfer reduced images over wireless network.
- Design and Implement multi-stage image compression algorithm in order to achieve more security over wireless network.
- Program and design a Graphical User Interface (GUI) of TCP/IP client and server sockets to send data across wireless network by using MATLAB program

1.4 Thesis Layout

This thesis is organized in five chapters; the remaining chapters can be summarized as follows:

- **Chapter 2**. Includes an overview of basic principle of iris pattern recognition, the concept of image compression by using PCA and wireless network system.
- **Chapter 3.** Focuses on the various design decisions that were made.
- **Chapter 4.** Discusses the software implementation results and the general discussion.
- **Chapter 5.** Includes the conclusions obtained from the implementation results followed by suggested future works.

Chapter Two

Theoretical Background

2.1 Introduction

This chapter explains the general introduction to biometrics, human iris and presents overview of three fields: iris pattern recognition system, image compression, and wireless network.

2.2 Biometrics and Human Iris

Biometrics is a set of methods used for automatic person identification based on their physiological and behavioral characteristics, such as fingerprint, face, iris, signature, hand, voice, DNA etc. Biometrics technology is simply make use of characteristics of humans to differentiate them from one another and it is more useful as compare to passwords and PIN numbers as they can be lost or stolen. A biometric system is a computer system that implements biometric recognition algorithms consisting of number of steps: firstly collection of biometric data, generating biometric template containing important features by using signal processing techniques, then matching current template to the stored templates, finally making decision about person's identity[17][18].

The iris is a thin circular diaphragm. The position of the iris lies in the center of the eye between the pupil and the sclera as showed in Fig. 2-1. The pupil is enclosed by the iris. The iris is used to control the amount of light is to be come into the eye. The human iris is a kind of physiological biometric feature. It contains unique important feature and it is reliable adequacy to be used as a biometric signature. Iris patterns are more unchangeable with time compared with other biometric features such as face and fingerprint [19] [20].

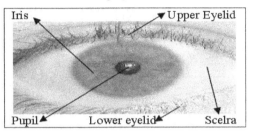

Figure 2-1 Human eye [19].

2.3   Iris Recognition System

Figure 2-2 illustrates the typical structure of an iris recognition system. The eye image sample is captured using a high resolution iris camera. After the capturing process and before the feature extraction in preprocessing stage, two steps need to be accomplished: iris localization of the captured image, and normalization that will transform segmented iris into predefined size. Then all the features achieved should enter the matching process to determine the user whose eye image was taken is who claimed to be [21].

2.3.1 Capturing Sample

The first stage of the iris recognition system is the image acquisition which is the most challenging and important stage and should be done accurately because having low quality sample will lead to failure into any of subsequent stages resulting in false identification. High resolution iris cameras with Near Infrared (NIR) illuminators are used for the purpose of samples capturing [18] [22].

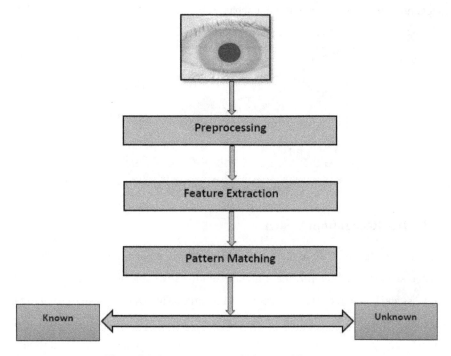

Figure 2-2 General structure of iris recognition system.

2.3.2 Iris Segmentation

The first preprocessing stage of the eye image obtained from the image acquisition stage is the iris localization. This process involves pupil and iris boundary detection, eyelid detection and removal of specular reflections. Several methods can be used to localize the portions of iris and the pupil from the eye image like Hough transformation, integrodifferential operator, Gradient based edge detection [23].

The Hough transform is a traditional and more popular extension technique used in many imaging applications for detecting lines in the image. Firstly, an edge map is built by computing the first derivatives of the intensity values in the eye image and then thresholding the result of it. For every set of parameters defining a curve that intersects at least one point on the edge map the Hough value is calculated. After that, the values are collected to build a Hough space where the highest value corresponds to a curve that intersects the biggest amount of edge points. These parameters are the center coordinates x_c and y_c , and the radius r, which are capable to declare any circle according to the following equation [18] [24]:

$$x^2{}_c + y_c{}^2 - r^2 = 0 \qquad \qquad \text{... (2.1)}$$

A maximum point in the Hough space will correspond to the radius and the center coordinates of the circle best expressed by the edge points. Kong and Wildes used parabolic Hough transform to obtain and separate the eyelids, approaching the top and bottom eyelids with parabolic arches, which are expressed as [24] [25]:

$$(-(x - h_j) \sin \theta_j + (y - k_j) \cos \theta_j)^2 = a_j((x - h_j) \cos \theta_j + (y - k_j) \sin \theta_j) \qquad \qquad \text{... (2.2)}$$

where a_j controls the curvature, (h_j, k_j) is the peak of the parabola and θ_j is the angle of rotation with respect to the x-axis.

2.3.3 Iris Normalization

The second preprocessing stage that map the extracted iris region into normalized form. The iris region need to be normalized to create a dimensionally consistent representation of the iris region in order to permit comparisons in the last stage of recognition because dimensional inconsistencies between iris regions are either due to the changes in distance between the eye and the image capturing device; differences in pupil sizes, caused by variations in illumination, which can cause the iris to dilate or contract [26] [27].

Normalization process uses a rubber sheet model, where the iris is modelled as a malleable rubber sheet which is unwrapped into a rectangular block with constant polar dimensions. In this model each point of the iris (x, y) is transformed into the dimensionless Polar coordinates (r, θ) ,where $0 < r \leq 1$ and $0 \leq \theta \leq 360°$ as shown in Fig. 2-3, has been modelled as [26]:

$$I\big(x(r,\theta), y(r,\theta)\big) \longrightarrow I(r,\theta) \qquad\qquad \text{... (2.3)}$$

With

$$x(r,\theta) = (1-r)x_p(\theta) + rx_i(\theta) \qquad\qquad \text{... (2.4)}$$

$$y(r,\theta) = (1-r)y_p(\theta) + ry_i(\theta) \qquad\qquad \text{... (2.5)}$$

where $I(x, y)$ is the iris image, (x, y) are the original Cartesian coordinates, (r, θ) are the corresponding normalized polar coordinates, and x_i, y_i and x_p, y_p are the coordinates of the iris and pupil confines along the θ direction.

The motivation behind the normalization process is to produce the iris areas with equal fixed dimensions, so that two images of the same iris picked up under changed conditions will have characteristic features at similar spatial location [26].

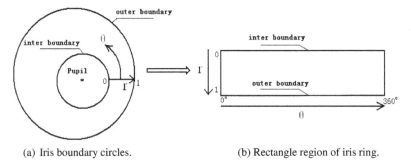

| (a) Iris boundary circles. | (b) Rectangle region of iris ring. |

Figure 2-3 Rubber sheet model [28].

2.3.4 Feature Encoding

In order to achieve the best recognition result, the encoding algorithm should extract the most discriminating information out of the iris. The following techniques are used to extract features from biometric pattern image.

2.3.4.1 1D Log-Gabor wavelets

This stage preforms extraction of iris features from normalized iris image and generating templates for further comparison. In order to achieve best or accurate recognition results of individuals, the most discriminating information existing in an iris pattern is extracted. Typically, methods including band-pass decomposition are used for creating a biometric template. Localized frequency information is extracted using 2D Gabor wavelets. Firstly, complex-valued coefficients that denote phases in a complex plane are computed. Then, depending on their location, vector angles are quantized to one of the four segments of a unit circle donating two bits into template [81] [29].

12

This encoding process is illustrated in Fig. 2-4, including both the demodulation and quantization, is defined as follows

$$h\{Re, Im\} = sgn_{\{Re, Im\}} \int_{\rho} \int_{\phi} I(\rho, \phi) \, e^{-i\omega(\theta_0 - \phi)} e^{-\frac{(r_0 - \rho)^2}{a^2}}$$

$$e^{-(\theta_0 - \phi)^2 / \beta^2} \rho \, d\rho \, d\phi \qquad\qquad ... (2.6)$$

where, h {Re, Im} has the real boundary and imaginary part, each having the value 1 or 0, depending on which quadrant it lies in. I (ρ, ϕ) is an iris image in polar coordinates as obtained from the previous stage (normalization process); a and β are the multiple-scale two dimensional wavelet size parameters, covering an 8-double range from 0.15 mm to 1.2 mm on the iris; ω is wavelet frequency, and (r_0, θ_0) are coordinates of the point for which the encoding is applied [81] [24].

Masek suggests Log-Gabor filter by convolving the normalized iris pattern with 1D Log-Gabor wavelets [29]:

$$G(f) = exp\left(\frac{-\left(log\left(\frac{f}{f_0}\right)\right)^2}{2\left(log\left(\frac{\sigma}{f_0}\right)\right)^2}\right) \qquad\qquad ... (2.7)$$

where f_0 denotes the center frequency of the filter, σ gives bandwidth of the filter. The 2D normalized pattern is divided into a number of 1D signals, and then these signals are convolved with 1D Gabor wavelet. The rows of the 2D normalized pattern are taken as the 1D signal. Every row corresponds to a circular ring on the iris region [18] [29].

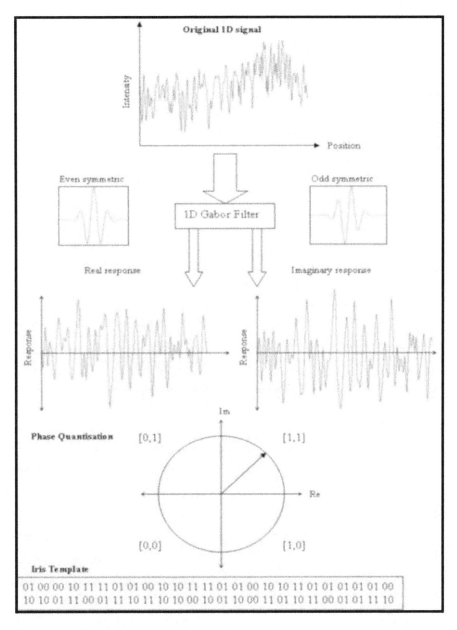

Figure 2-4 Feature encoding process [24].

2.3.4.2 Genetic Algorithm

Genetic algorithms are optimization methods that search for best solution to the problem under consideration until a particular ending condition is met. The solution to a problem is called a chromosome. The parameters to be optimized are called genes, which are the contents of the chromosome. The basic parts that are prevalent to almost every genetic algorithm are shown below (see Fig. 2-5) [30] [31]:

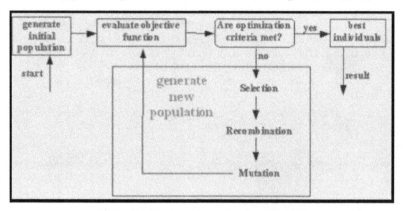

Figure 2-5 Structure of Genetic Algorithm [30].

- Initial population: which it is set of chromosomes that randomly chosen in the beginning of the algorithm and this collection will be serve as the first generation [31].
- Fitness or evaluation function for optimization: this function is the most important component of the algorithm because it tests and quantifies how to fit each potential solution. The chromosome refers to a numeric value that symbolize a candidate solution to the problem. Each candidate solution is

15

encoded as an array of values. If a problem has N_{pr} dimensions, then classically every chromosome is encoded as an N_{pr}-element array [31].

$$chromosome = [p_1, p_2, \dots, p_{N_{pr}}] \qquad \dots (2.8)$$

Where each p_i is a specific value (gene) of the ith parameter.

- Selection operator: To reach an acceptable solution, a population must run through several generations. At each generation selection operator selects some of the chromosomes for reproduction based on a probability distribution defined by the user. The more fitter a chromosome is, it is likely to be selected [30] [31].

    Roulette wheel selection is common used selection algorithm that contains few steps, at first it computes the total fitness of population [32]:

$$F = \sum_{i=1}^{population\ size} evaluate(v_i) \qquad \dots (2.9)$$

Then calculates the probability of selection P_i for each individual v_i [32]:

$$P_i = \frac{evaluate(v_i)}{F} \qquad \dots (2.10)$$

Finally, finds the cumulative probability Q_i for each individual v_i. Then generate random number f from the range $[0..1]$ if($f < Q_1$) then individual v_1 will be selected, otherwise i^{th} individual v_i is selected ($2 \leq i \leq$ *Population Size*) such that $Q_{i-1} < f \leq Q_i$ [32] [33].

$$Q_i = \sum_{j=1}^{i} P_j \qquad \dots (2.11)$$

- Recombination: Recombination merges or crossed over parts of two or more parent's solutions to create new generation, perhaps better solutions (i.e. offspring). Cross over operator exchange a part of the sequence of the two

16

selected chromosomes to produce two offspring. For example, if the parent chromosomes are [31] [33]:

[11110111001110] and [01011101010011]

Are crossed over after the fourth bit, then the new offspring are;

[01010111001110] and [11111101010011]

- Mutation operator: flips individual bits in the new chromosomes at random turning 0 to 1 and vice versa. Mutation may be applied to offspring achieved by crossover at random to any individual in the population [31] [34]. For example, if the mutation is applied to the offspring produced by the cross over operation;

[01010111001110] and [11111101010011]

If the mutation happens after the fourth bit, then the new offspring are;

[01011111001110] and [11110101010011]

The selection, crossover, and mutation processes continues until the number of offspring is equal to the initial generation, so that the second generation is consists entirely of new offspring and the first generation is completely replaced [31].

2.3.5 Pattern Matching

The final stage of the iris recognition system that preforms comparisons between two iris templates. Template of input person or individual is compared with stored templates to determine whether the input template originates from an authenticated person or an imposter. The matching process can be calculated using different metrics like Hamming Distance. Hamming Distance is a measure of how many bits are identical between two bits patterns. Using the Hamming Distance of two bit patterns, a decision depend on whether the two patterns were achieved from dissimilar Irises or from the same one. In comparing the bit patterns X and Y, the

17

Hamming Distance (HD), is defined as the sum of disagreeing bits over N, the total number of bits in the feature vectors and is given by the Equation [35] [36]:

$$HD = \frac{1}{N}\sum_{J=1}^{N} X_J \oplus Y_J \qquad \qquad ... (2.12)$$

2.3.6 Iris Recognition Performance Measurements

Three measurements named; False Acceptance Rate (FAR), False Rejection Rate (FRR) and Correct Recognition Rate (CRR) were considered to measure the performance of iris recognition systems [18]. FAR is the probability that a biometric system will incorrectly identify an individual,

$$FAR = \frac{number\ of\ falsely\ accepted\ people}{number\ of\ all\ presented\ attempts} \qquad ... (2.13)$$

The FRR is the probability that a biometric system will fail to identify an individual,

$$FRR = \frac{number\ of\ falsely\ rejected\ poeple}{number\ of\ all\ presented\ attempts} \qquad ... (2.14)$$

And the CRR is used to measure how many input individuals that the system correctly identify from the all individuals attempts,

$$CRR = \frac{number\ of\ correctly\ accepted\ poeple}{number\ of\ all\ presented\ attempts} \qquad ... (2.15)$$

2.4 Image Compression

Image is an array or matrix of square pixels organized in the form of rows and columns. An image is a picture which contains highly redundant and irrelevant information which is stored in an electronic form. Data compression methods becomes more and more important for reducing the data redundancy to save more

18

hardware space and transmission bandwidth. In computer science, data compression method is the process of encoding information using fewer bits [37] [38].

2.4.1 Image Compression Using PCA

Principal component analysis (PCA) has been widely applied in the area of image compression. PCA belongs to linear transforms based on the statistical techniques. PCA has been applied as standalone image compression and data dimension reduction techniques as well as pre-processing or post-processing step in combination with several other techniques [39] [40].

PCA can be used as image reduction method in order to reduced image size. Firstly, any RGB image must be converted to gray scale image, the gray image format is $row * col$ matrix. Then, gray image matrix is centered by computing the mean of the image matrix I, then subtracting each pixel gray value from the mean gray value [41].

$$MeanI = \frac{1}{row*col} \sum_{r=1}^{row} \sum_{c=1}^{col} I(r,c) \qquad ... (2.16)$$

$$Centered\ Image\ CI(r,c) = \sum_{r=1}^{row} \sum_{c=1}^{col} (MeanI - I(r,c)) \qquad ... (2.17)$$

Then the covariance of the CI is computed as follows [44],

$$CovImg(r,c) = CI(r,c) * CI(r,c)^T \qquad ... (2.18)$$

where $CI(r,c)^T$ is the transpose of the matrix $CI(r,c)$. The Eigen values and Eigen vectors of the covariance matrix is computed as follows,

$$A.V = \lambda.V \qquad ... (2.19)$$

Where A is m*m (gray scale matrix), V is m*1 (non-zero Eigen vector), and λ is a scalar (Eigen value). Any value of λ for which the above equation has a solution is named the Eigen value of A and the vector V which coincides to this value is named the Eigen vector of A [41].

$$A.V - \lambda.I.V = 0$$
$$(A - \lambda.I).V = 0 \qquad \qquad ...\,(2.20)$$

The roots of $|A - \lambda.I|$ will give the Eigen values and for every Eigen value there will be an Eigen vector. The biggest Eigen values and the correspondent Eigen vectors are taken out to form the principal components of the image (centered image). Finally, based on the principal components, the image can be split up into various Eigen vectors as follows [41]:

$$Image = \begin{bmatrix} Eigen\ vector_1 \\ Eigen\ vector_2 \\ Eigen\ vector_3 \\ ... \end{bmatrix} \qquad \qquad ...\,(2.21)$$

2.4.2 Image Quality Measurements

The performance of the image compression technique is evaluated by measuring compression efficiency and image quality. The compression efficiency is measured by using Compression Ratio (CR) [42],

$$CR = \frac{size\ of\ original\ image}{size\ of\ compressed\ image} \qquad \qquad ...\,(2.22)$$

The CR is usually below 2 for lossless compression, but ranging from 2 up to 10 for lossy compression. Achieving high CR, will result of less quality of reconstructed images and vice versa. The Peak Signal to Noise Ratio (PSNR) was used to evaluate the reconstructed image quality. The PSNR in decibels (dB) is defined as follows [43] [44],

$$PSNR = \frac{peakval^2}{MSE} \qquad \qquad \dots (2.23)$$

Where $peakval$ is either given by the user or taken from the range of the image data type. For example, if the input matrix has a double precision floating point data type, then $peakval$ is 1, or if it has 8-bit unsigned integer data type $peakval$ is 255, etc. And the MSE is the Mean Square Error between input image and reconstructed image, the MSE is defined as follows [44],

$$MSE = \frac{\sum_{M,N}[I_1(m,n)-I_2(m,n)]^2}{M*N} \qquad \qquad \dots (2.24)$$

Where M and N are the numbers of rows and columns in the input image matrix respectively. The input uncompressed image is $I_1(m,n)$ and the reconstructed image is $I_2(m,n)$. The standard values for the PSNR in lossy image compression are between 30 and 50 dB for 8-bit data, where higher is better. For 16-bit data, the typical values for the PSNR are between 60 and 80 dB, for 32-bit are ranging from 90 and 110 dB, and for 64-bit data are between 120 and 140. Higher PSNR means that the resulted reconstructed image has good quality and lower error introduced [43].

2.5   Wireless Network System

Wireless networks are becoming progressively popular because of the availability of inexpensive hardware and the essential benefit it has for the user over wired networks. The demand for connecting devices without using cables is increasing everywhere. Wireless networks offer many advantages over fixed or wired networks like mobility, flexibility, and easier to use [45] [46].

A network is set of hardware and software devices connected by communication links such as a wire cable or radio link. The categories in which computer networks in general falls into are; LAN, WAN, MAN, where Local Area Networks (LANs) are designed to allow resources to be shared between personal computers, and Wide Area Network (WAN) offers long range of data transmission across large geographic areas, and Metropolitan Area Network (MAN) which covers area with size between LAN and WAN such as town or city [47].

2.6.1 Wireless Network Architectures

There are two common types of wireless architectures: infrastructure and ad hoc networks. The wireless network in which network stations communicate with each other by first going through an access point (AP) is called infrastructure network as shown in Fig. 2-6. Stations can communicate with each other wirelessly or via wire [48].

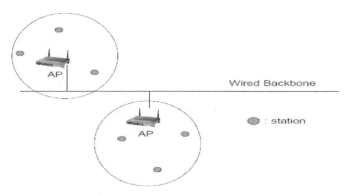

Figure 2-6 Infrastructure network [48].

When the stations of wireless network communicate directly with each other, without the use of an AP is called an ad hoc network as shown in Fig. 2-7. Ad hoc networks are beneficial in the cases that temporary network connectivity is desired [48].

22

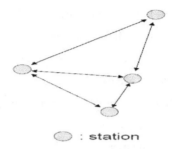

⬭ : station

Figure 2-7 Ad hoc network [48].

2.6.2 Network communication

The main method of network communication is using TCP/IP communication protocol suit that makes use of network sockets to transfer data between devices of the network bi-directionally. In this manner, the computer that is controlling the relay can send commands and shortly thereafter receive the response through the same Socket. In most programming languages, firstly a socket must opened to import the appropriate plug-in, then build the socket object, and connect the socket using the IP Address and Port Number of the target device. The concept of IP addressing, that means that it provides an IP address to every machine on the network in order to deliver data packets, and Port Numbers are basically the entry into a network or device that allow access to its internals from remote communications [49] [50]. IP address and port number play very important role in selecting the final destination of data. After the host is selected by using IP address of it, then the port number defines one of process on that particular host as shown in Fig. 2-8 [47].

23

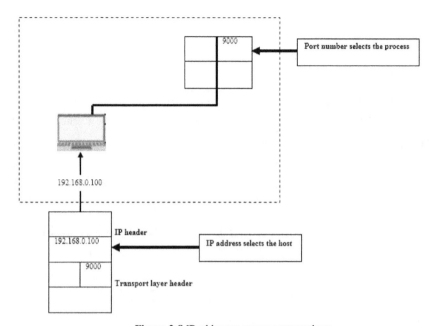

Figure 2-8 IP addresses verses port numbers.

2.6.3 Network monitoring

To control any network, the network administrator needs to monitor that network. Network monitoring is a difficult process, which it's a demanding task that is an important part of a network manager job. Network monitoring is not only involved with the monitoring of the physical network equipment such as routers, and computers, but also involved with the monitoring of services which are executing on these devices. The services offer data storage, management, communication services and they are executing in the network Layer and above. There are two Monitoring Techniques; Router Based and Non-Router Based, where routers by themselves preform network monitoring, without the need of any additional hardware or

24

software installation. Non router based techniques demand for an extra hardware and software to be installed to provide greater flexibility [51] [52].

The most widely used tools of router based monitoring techniques are; Simple Network Monitoring Protocol (SNMP), and Remote Monitoring (RMON). Non router based monitoring techniques is also classified in to three methods such as Active Monitoring, Passive Monitoring and Combinational Monitoring. In Active monitoring probes are transmitted into the network to gather measurements between at least two terminal points in the network. The generally used tools such as ping utility, which measures the lateness and loss of packets, and trace route which helps determine topology of the network. (Internet Control Message Protocol (ICMP) packets (probes) are sent to the specified host and wait for the host to reply back to the sender as shown in Fig. 2-9. Passive monitoring is different from active monitoring, because it collects information about only one point in the network. While Combinational Monitoring, utilizes the preferable characteristics of both passive and active monitoring [51] [53].

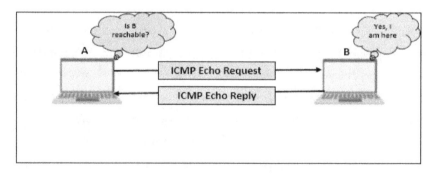

Figure 2-9 ICMP (ping) command.

Chapter Three

Hardware and Software Design

3.1 Introduction

This chapter is divided into three parts; the first part explains iris recognition components with two feature extraction methods which are implemented using MATLAB2015a program and introduces system performance measurement, the second part implements image compression-decompression using PCA (principal component analysis) as data reduction method, and the third part discusses the implantation of the wireless network system. The complete system road map is shown in the Fig. 3-1 according to the section number.

3.2 General system architecture

The system architecture is shown in Fig. 3-2. The network administrator (the user of central Personal Computer (PC)) selects iris image from the Chinese Academy of Sciences Institute of Automation (CASIA) database and also selects the type of iris pattern recognition method used on each line of the proposed network. Network monitoring and controlling takes place in the central PC. All recognition results are sent back to the central pc and the network administrator takes the final decision of these results.

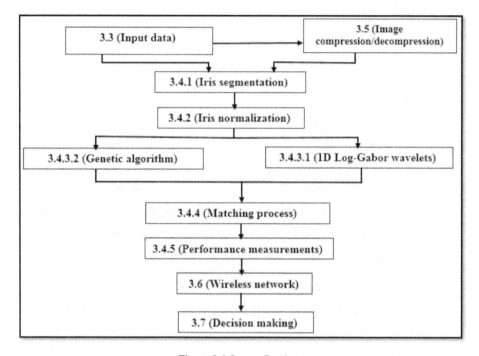

Figure 3-1 System Road map.

This system consists of the following hardware and software parts. The hardware used in the system consists of two parts:

- Wireless and wired communication
- Personal computers

The software used in the system consists of:

- MATLAB program version (R2015a) to make GUI which is responsible for the main operation of the PC.
- NetSupport School Professional software version (10.70.5) [54], which is responsible for network monitoring and controlling.

27

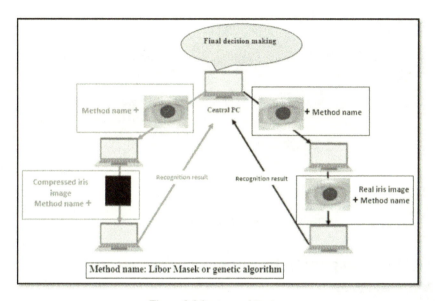

Figure 3-2 System architecture.

3.3 Input Data

Input data is obtained from CASIA iris database, publicly provided by Chinese Academy of Sciences. CASIA database is widely used by many researchers and developers for the purpose of testing iris recognition systems. The database consists of 756 high resolution gray scale images with resolution of 320*280 pixels stored in BMP format. These images were captured by means of IR iris camera. Images were taken from 108 different persons and 7 images were captured for each person in two sessions as shown in Fig. 3-3.

28

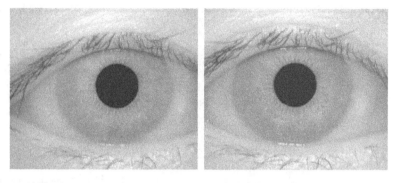

| (a) Session one. | (b) Session two. |

Figure 3-3 Example from CASIA_IrisV1 database [55].

3.4   Main components of The Iris Recognition System

3.4.1 Iris Segmentation

The input eye image is segmented using circular Hough transform to detect iris and pupil boundaries (circles) as shown in Fig. 3-4. Circular Hough transform is implemented by employing canny edge detection. In order to make circle detection more effective and precise iris and pupil radiuses has to be set according to the database used. For CASIA database, the range for iris radius is [95-150] pixels, while the range for pupil radius is [28-75] pixels. After both circles (iris and pupil boundaries) has been detected, six parameters are stored, the radius, x and y center of both circles.

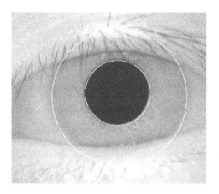

Figure 3-4 Segmentation with circles of 002_2_4 image from CASIA database.

Eyelids are detected using linear Hough transform by fitting a line to the upper and lower eyelids then second straight line is drawn which intersects with first line at the iris edge. Eyelashes detection is performed by simple thresholding as shown in Fig. 3-5. Thresholding is possible when only the eyelashes is dark and no other details has low intensity.

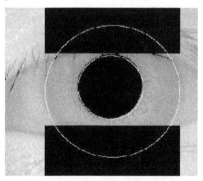

Figure 3-5 Noise removal by isolating eyelashes and eyelids.

3.4.2 Iris normalization

Iris normalization is implemented using Daugman's rubber sheet model that performs normalization of the iris region by unwrapping the circular region as shown in Fig. 3-6 into a rectangular block of constant dimensions. Two values need to be set manually in order to be used later in the normalization process: angular resolution and radial resolution. 20 is chosen for angular resolution (number of data points are selected along each radial line) and 240 for radial resolution (number of radial lines going around the iris area) as iris normalization area. The output of the normalization process is 2D vectors with angular resolution at horizontal direction and radial resolution at vertical direction. The first vector of Fig. 3-7, is the normalized iris region which contains the segmented iris region and the second one, is the noise region which holds the regions that contain reflections and the eyelids and eyelashes detected in the segmentation process previously. Pixels that are set to 1 in the second vector are not included in the calculations of encoding and matching processes.

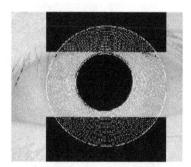

Figure 3-6 Iris region with virtual concentric circles.

31

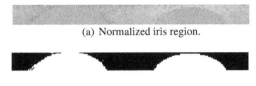

(a) Normalized iris region.

(b) Normalized noise region.

Figure 3-7 Iris normalization process.

3.4.3 Feature Extraction

3.4.3.1   1D Log-Gabor wavelets

The encoding process takes the normalized iris and treats each row of it as 1D signal, each row corresponds to particular circular ring around the iris region. Then these 1D signals are convolved using 1D log-Gabor wavelets as shown in Fig. 2-4 and Fig. 3-8 that illustrates encoding process steps. The information at the angular direction is taken because it provides more independence rather than at radial direction of the normalized iris.

The output of the convolution process is quantized using four level phase quantization. Each filter produces two bit of data for each phasor. In order to reduce the number of discordant bits in the resulting templates, grey code is used, so that the difference between neighboring quadrants is only one bit. The outputs of the encoding process are iris template and noise mask in which iris template contains a number of bits of important iris information and the corresponding noise mask holds corrupted areas within the iris region as shown in Fig. 3-9. In order to remove trivial information, regions that results with phase amplitude ≤ 0 must be marked in the noise mask.

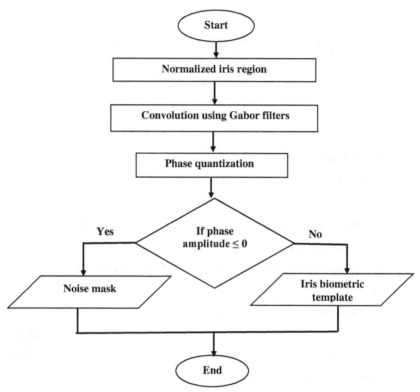

Figure 3-8 Flowchart of the encoding process, by using 1D Log-Gabor wavelet.

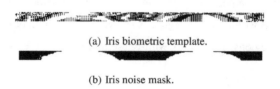

(a) Iris biometric template.

(b) Iris noise mask.

Figure 3-9 Outputs of the encoding process, by using 1D Log-Gabor wavelet.

3.4.3.2 Genetic Algorithm Optimization Method

Genetic algorithm is used to maximize finding the best matching score between individuals. In the beginning of the process, the algorithm generates initial population (G0) randomly with number of individuals as the input to the algorithm. Then, compute the matching score for the individuals of the population as shown in Fig. 3-10, and the matching score is expressed in following equation,

$$Score = \frac{correct\ match}{total\ match} \qquad \qquad \text{... (3.1)}$$

To create the next generation (G_k) where $k = 1,\dots m$ and m is the size of generation, the following four steps required to be applied to the individuals of the current population:

1. Selection step: the individuals with the maximum similarity score (highest fitness value) are kept unaltered and likely to be selected as parents for the next generation as a part of the selection process. The best score between individuals is selected once every 50 iteration. The lower fitness value is returned until highest fitness value is found.

2. Crossover step: parents are combined to form the children for the next generation by using crossover method with rate equals to 100% fixed over all generation, which means that all children are made by crossover operator , where crossover rate or crossover probability is the ratio of how many couples will be picked for mating process.

3. Mutation step: random changes are applied to the new children by the mutation process with rate equals to less than 20%, where mutation rate or mutation probability is a measure of the likeness that random bits of children will be flipped from 0 to 1 and vice versa.

4. Decision step: if the number of new offspring of the current generation is not the same as initial generation then return to step1.

The algorithm stops when the maximum number of iterations (generations) exceeded or when the best fitness score of the individuals in the population is higher than 0.800.

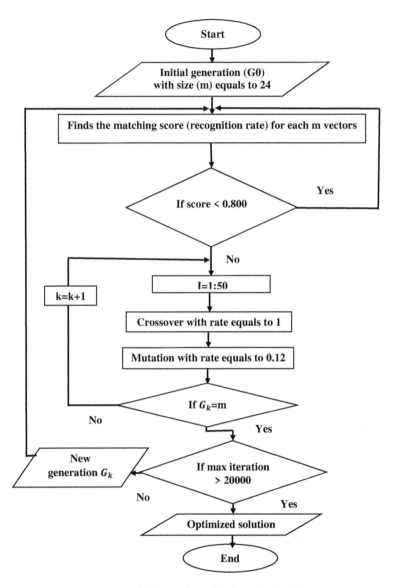

Figure 3-10 Flowchart of the genetic algorithm process.

3.4.4 Matching Process

Comparisons between individual's irises is performed by using Hamming Distance (HD) measuring metric [56],

$$HD = \frac{\|(templatex \otimes templatey) \cap maskx \cap masky\|}{\|maskx \cap masky\|} \qquad \dots (3.2)$$

The comparison occurs between input (templates, masks) and stored (templates, masks) as shown in Fig 3-11, then the result of the comparison is tested with threshold value which equals to 0.3834. When the value of HD is less than 0.3834, the decision is known otherwise the decision will be unknown for the current person.

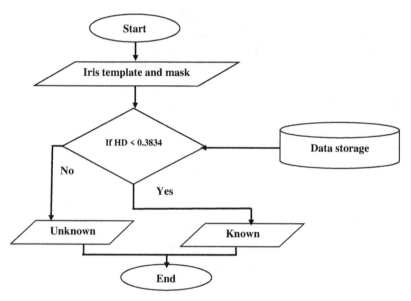

Figure 3-11 Matching process of Mask algorithm.

3.5 Image Compression/Decompression

3.5.1 One-Stage Image Compression

Principal Component Analysis (PCA) is used as dimension reduction method by reducing the number of dimension with low errors. PCA takes input image matrix in the beginning and finds the mean of it. Then finds the covariance matrix and computes the eigenvectors (principal components) and collect them into projection matrix. Each of those eigenvectors is associated with an eigenvalue, which is the size or dimension of the corresponding eigenvector. The eigenvalues is arranged in descending order and the eigenvectors are chosen corresponding to the largest eigenvalues. Finally, the final matrix is constructed from the selected eigenvectors as shown in Fig. 3-12 that illustrates PCA algorithm steps in detail.

The image is decompressed by preforming Inverse Principal Components Analysis (IPCA) on the compressed image as shown in Fig. 3-13. The IPCA algorithm starts by computing the inverse of eigenvectors matrix, then multiply the inverse matrix by compressed image matrix. The decompressed image matrix is constructed by adding the mean matrix to the transpose of the multiplication.

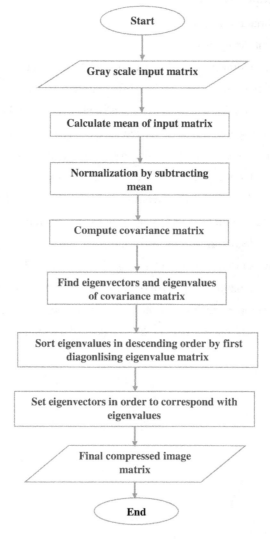

Figure 3-12 PCA algorithm.

39

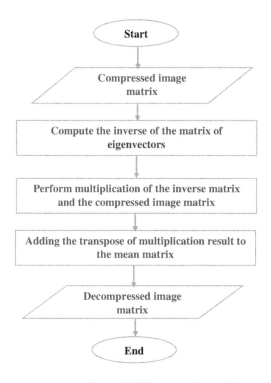

Figure 3-13 IPCA algorithm.

3.5.2 The Proposed Multi-Stage Image Compression

A new algorithm is proposed to compress image at many different stages, it's a sequence of image compression stages. With each stage, there is a new different compressed image that has different size. These sequence of image compression stages are corresponding to the decreasing of image sizes. The process is called the forward multi-stage image compression. The reverse direction or the backward multi-stage image compression contains a sequence of image decompression stages, which are corresponding to the increasing of image sizes. This technique is applied to the iris images of the CASIA database. Iris images is compressed N times reaching to constant image size as shown in Fig. 3.14 below, Where N is equals to 9 and the final image size is equals to 1kB. N is equals to 9 because this is the last compression stage where image size cannot change anymore and settle on 1kB.

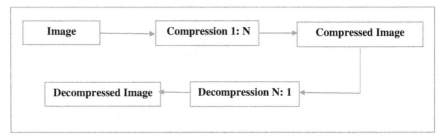

Figure 3.14 multi-stage image compression/decompression.

For more security, this technique can be used in networks to protect transmitted data from hackers because hackers cannot guess how much the image has been compressed. So this method can be considered as a security technique.

3.6 Wireless Network

Each network system consists of hardware and software subsystems. The following section discusses the design of those subsystems.

3.6.1 Proposed Network's Hardware Design

Networking hardware includes all equipment needed to perform data processing and communications within the network. In the Fig. 3-15, the proposed network consists of 5 Personal Computers (PCs), each Personal Computer (PC) communicates with one another through an access point. The access point used in this network is TL-

WR741ND router with one detachable antenna, this device provides combined wired/wireless network connection integrated with one WLAN port and 4-LAN ports as shown in Fig 3-16. In the proposed wireless network, PC1, PC2 and PC3 is connected to the router using Ethernet-LAN cables, while both of PC2 and PC3 are connected wirelessly with PC4 and PC5 respectively. Bridge connection is used in order for PC2 and PC3 to be connected to PC4 and PC5 respectively.

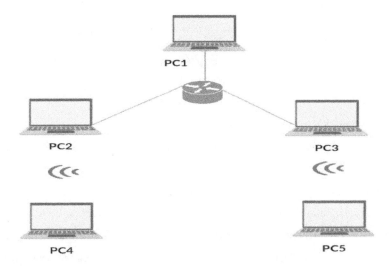

Figure 3-15 Proposal wireless network hardware system.

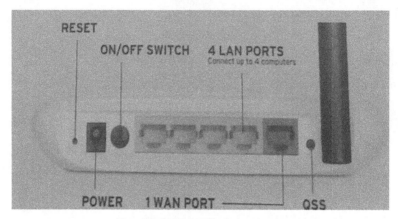

Figure 3-16 TP-LINK wireless router.

3.6.2 Network's Software Design

The proposed network system consists of five PCs, all of network's PCs transfer data by using Transmission Control Protocol/Internet Protocol (TCP/IP), which is programmed using the network role property of MATLAB program. TCP requires only the destination's IP address and port number for the data to be transferred to that destination. Client and server TCP sockets are programmed using the network role property on the TCP/IP interface that support a single remote connection. To communicate over TCP/IP interface, TCP/IP object must be created before transmission with remote host's IP address and port number. The Port number must be a positive integer between 1 and 65535. The typical workflow for TCP/IP server and TCP/IP client sessions is shown in Fig. 3-17 and Fig. 3-18 respectively. In the server session, after server socket is opened, the server will wait until an incoming connection is established. In client session, the received data have to be reshaped to their original data size. The time out for the writing and reading operations can be

43

determined in both sessions. IP's of network's PCs have to be set up statically or dynamically before network transmission takes place. Static IP addressing is applied on the proposal network because it provides more reliability than dynamic IP addressing. The network transfers iris image into two lines as shown in Fig. 3-19. In the first line, PC1 sends input image to PC2, then PC2 will compress the image and send it to PC4. Then PC4 decompresses the image and send the result of recognition back to PC1 wirelessly as shown in Fig. 3-19. In the second line, PC1 sends the same input image to PC3, then PC3 will send the same image without compression to PC5. Then PC5 send the result of recognition back to PC1 also via wireless. After receiving both results (from PC4 and PC5) PC1 will compare between these two results in order to make the final decision.

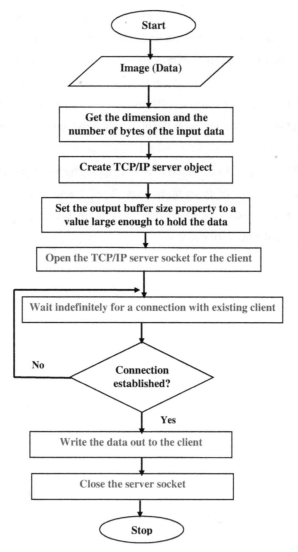

Figure 3-17 TCP/IP server session.

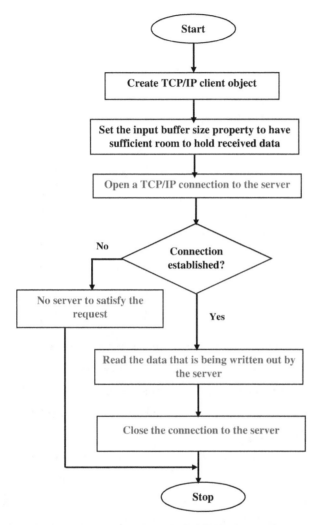

Figure 3-18 TCP/IP client session.

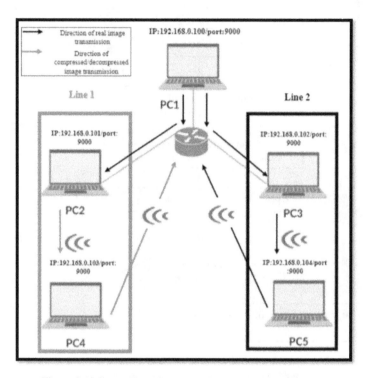

Figure 3-19 Proposal wireless network system communication.

The overall wireless network is controlled and monitored in PC1 (central PC) using NetSupport School software program, by setting the central PC (PC1) as a teacher and the rest of network PC'S as students. If all students are connected properly, the teacher will starts the classroom of all connected students. To make sure that all students are connected properly to the central PC, ICMP ping utility is used to discover the connected and disconnected PCs. Ping utility only needs the destination's IP address to test a connection. When replay is returned from the specified destination, means that the destination is properly connected into the network as shown in Fig. 3-20.

47

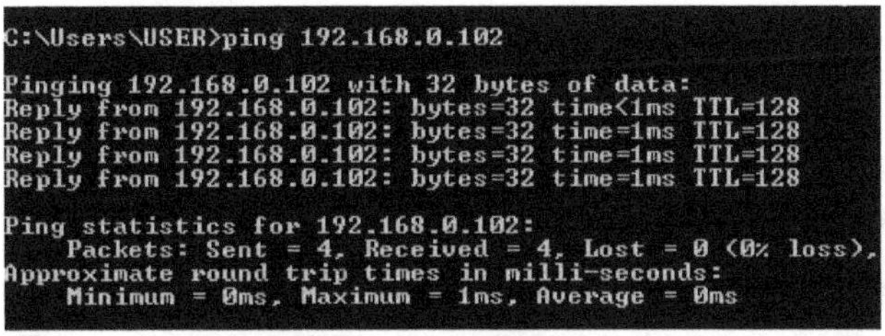

```
C:\Users\USER>ping 192.168.0.102

Pinging 192.168.0.102 with 32 bytes of data:
Reply from 192.168.0.102: bytes=32 time<1ms TTL=128
Reply from 192.168.0.102: bytes=32 time=1ms TTL=128
Reply from 192.168.0.102: bytes=32 time=1ms TTL=128
Reply from 192.168.0.102: bytes=32 time=1ms TTL=128

Ping statistics for 192.168.0.102:
    Packets: Sent = 4, Received = 4, Lost = 0 (0% loss),
Approximate round trip times in milli-seconds:
    Minimum = 0ms, Maximum = 1ms, Average = 0ms
```

Figure 3-20 PC1 sending ping request to PC3.

3.7 Decision Making

It is the role of the network administrator is to take the final decision of the received recognition results. If one recognition result was different from the other of the same input image for both network lines, then the network administrator will selects another iris image sample of the same person for transmission and test the results one more time. The final decisions is shown in Table 3-1

Table 3-1 Final decision making.

Recognition result from line 1	Recognition result from line 2	Final decision
Correct match	Correct match	Correct match
False match	Correct match	False match (input another image)
Correct match	False match	False match (input another image)
False match	False match	False match

48

Chapter Four

System Implementation Results and Discussion

4.1 Introduction

In this chapter, the obtained results are presented. The graphical and text descriptions of the application Graphical User Interface (GUI) are also given. Three work cases are presented in this chapter. The first is the case where two methods of iris pattern recognition are presented for comparison based on accuracy and computation time. In the second case, the compression of iris images implied in order to reduce their size for later network transmission. The third case, network transmission time is computed for both compressed and uncompressed iris images by using the two methods of iris pattern recognition.

4.2 System requirement

To setup the proposed system, few requirements must be met. The following software and hardware are to be installed:

- Windows version 7 and above.
- MATLAB program version (R2015a/8.5).
- NetSupport School Professional software version (10.70.5).
- Lenovo B570e, CORE i3 laptop.
- Lenovo G480, CORE i5 laptop.
- Lenovo G570, CORE i3 laptop.
- Acer AOD257, CORE i3 notebook.
- Toshiba Portege M780, CORE i5 laptop.
- Three of UTP cat-6 network cables.

- TL-WR741ND 150Mbps wireless N router version (4.25).

4.3 Iris Pattern Recognition Methods Comparison

Two methods are presented in this research; Libor Masek method and modified genetic method. These two methods are tested by using CASIA database, which contains 108 classes, each class consists of 7 image samples. Four images are used for training and three for testing. The input test image template is compared with all 432 (108*4) stored image templates in case of 108 classes (see Appendix A), and 200 (50*4) in case of 50 classes, and 100 (25*4) in case of 25 classes. GUIs are shown in Fig. 4-1, and Fig. 4-2 for Libor Masek method and genetic method respectively.

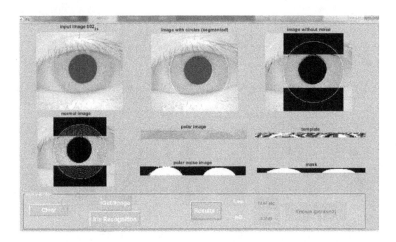

Figure 4-1 GUI result of Libor Masek method for 002-2-4 image of CASIA database.

To measure the accuracy of the two methods, FAR, FRR and CRR are used into two cases. The first case, the accuracy is measured for persons (each person

50

contains three image samples) and the second case is measured for samples (each sample means one image). The accuracy measurements for persons and samples are shown in the Table 4-1and Table 4-2 respectively.

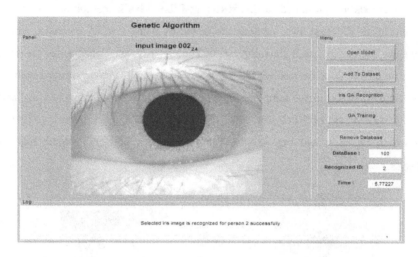

Figure 4-2 GUI result of genetic method for 002-2-4 image of CASIA database.

Table 4-1: Accuracy results for persons.

No. of persons	Masek algorithm			Genetic algorithm		
	FAR%	FRR%	CRR%	FAR%	FRR%	CRR%
25	0.00	0.00	100	0.00	0.00	100
50	0.00	0.00	100	0.00	0.00	100
108	0.00	0.00	100	0.00	0.00	100

Table 4-2: Accuracy results for samples.

No. of samples	Masek algorithm			Genetic algorithm		
	FAR%	FRR%	CRR%	FAR%	FRR%	CRR%
75	0.00	1.33	98.66	0.00	0.00	100
150	0.00	1.33	98.66	0.66	0.66	99.33
324	0.00	4.93	95.06	1.54	2.77	97.22

The Table 4-1 shows the comparison of Masek and genetic algorithms in performance for three groups of persons, where three testing image samples are taken for each person. In the used methods, at least one image sample is correct matched for each person which makes zero error rate and 100% recognition rate because there is no person in all groups that is false accepted or false rejected.

For more details, the Masek and genetic algorithms are compared for three groups of samples as shown in Table 4-2. The results shows that the error rate (FAR, FRR) is increases when the number of samples increase, and the recognition rate decreases when more samples are included. Genetic method has achieved higher correct recognition rates than Masek method.

4.4 Image Compression/Decompression

4.4.1 One-Stage Image Compression/Decompression

The main reason of compression is to reduce the size of data while keeping the important information. PCA is used as data reduction method to compress the size of image while maintaining the useful information. The compressed image is returned back to their original form, by using IPCA with losing very low amount of information, while keeping image quality is almost as the same as original image. GUI for PCA method is shown in the Fig. 4-3.

The quality of reconstructed images are measured by using compression ratio and PSNR (see Appendix B). The average compression ratios are ranging from 3.04 to 3.29, for all three samples of the first 25 CASIA classes as shown in Fig. 4-4, which shows compression ratios among all 25 samples is less than 10. Lower compression ratios means higher quality of reconstructed images. The PSNRs is also measured for 25 samples, which are ranging from 298.51 to 301.47 as shown in Fig. 4-5. The

PSNR is evaluated for 64-bit double-precision floating-point images. The reconstructed images are of good quality, which are the same as original image because of the low CRs and high PSNRs with low error introduced.

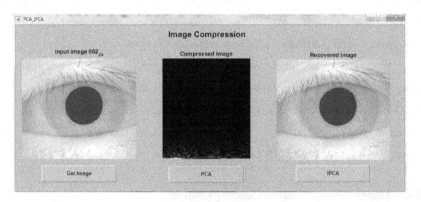

Figure 4-3 PCA compression/decompression of 002-2-4 image of CASIA database.

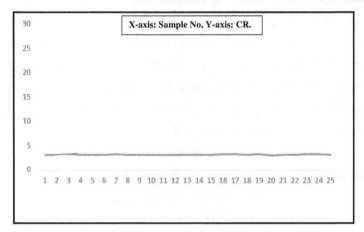

Figure 4-4 Compression ratios of 25 image samples.

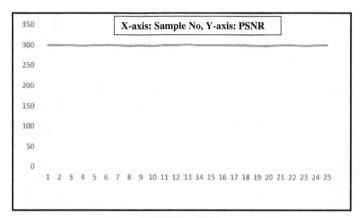

Figure 4-5 PSNRs of 25 image samples.

4.4.2 Multi-Stage Image Compression/Decompression

In this technique, PCA is performed 9 times on the input iris image. In the beginning the input image is selected, and the compression index is assigned to each stage, the appropriate GUI for multi-stage compression is shown in Fig. 4-6.

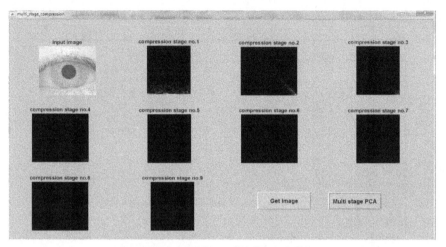

Figure 4-6 GUI for Multi-Stage compression.

4.5   Wireless Network

The most important factor in networks in general is transmission time. LAN networks transmits faster than wireless network, so including LAN cables in wireless networks can help to make the overall network performs more faster than wireless. The proposed wireless network is monitored in the teacher PC (PC1). After the software is opened and starts as classroom, the software will scan for all available students, then add them to the specified room. The teacher PC has a full control on all the available students in the network, so any disconnected student from the network will disappear from the teacher screen. The teacher PC can also have the knowledge of which PC's are connected via wire or wirelessly. The netsupport school teacher screen for the proposed wireless network is shown in Fig. 4-7.

The teacher PC runs two MATLAB sessions in addition to network monitoring, each session transmits image for specific network line. PC1 sends input eye image that is selected by user to either PC2 or PC3. The final iris recognition results is sent back to PC1 from PC4 or PC5. The designed GUI for the two sessions in PC1 is shown in Fig. 4-8. Every network transmission process is executed by using TCP/IP server sockets and every network reception process is executed by using TCP/IP client sockets.

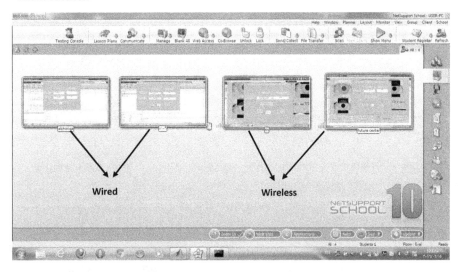

Figure 4-7 Netsupport school teacher's screen.

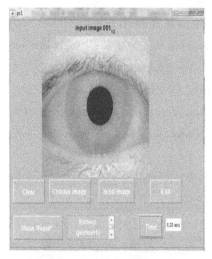
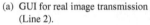
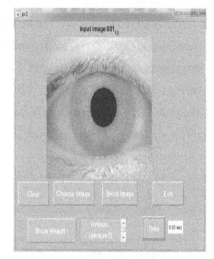

(a) GUI for real image transmission
(Line 2).

(b) GUI for compressed/decompressed
image transmission (Line 1).

Figure 4-8 Two MATLAB sessions in PC1.

In PC1, after transmitting input image, the method for iris recognition is determined. The GUI for method selection is shown in the Fig. 4-9.

From PC1 by controlling PC2, the compressed image plus compression parameters are sent from PC2 to PC4. The GUI for PC2 reception and transmission is shown in Fig. 4-10. When Multi-stage image compression is performed for the received input image (see Fig. 4-6), all compressed images is stored at PC2. Then the user will select the compressed image wanted to be sent to PC4. Compression Index (CI) of the selected compressed image in additional to the compressed image will be sent to PC4, the appropriate GUI for PC2 performing multi-stage image compression is shown in Fig. 4-11.

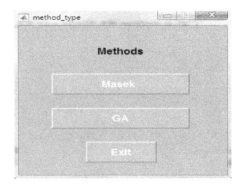

Figure 4-9 GUI for iris recognition method selection.

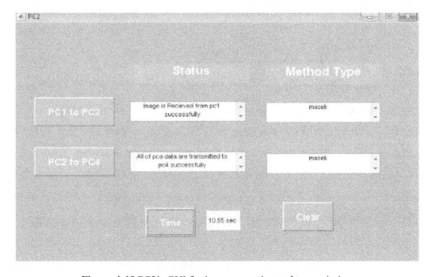

Figure 4-10 PC2's GUI for image reception and transmission.

58

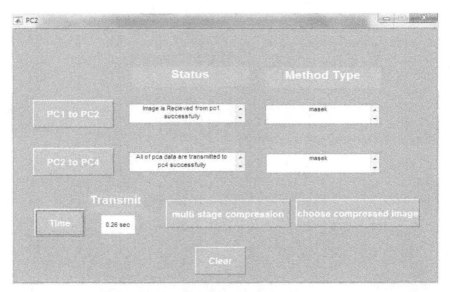

Figure 4-11 PC2's GUI for multi-stage image compression.

In PC1 also by opening PC3 client or student screen, the image that is received From PC1 is transmitted the same to PC5. PC3 GUI is shown in Fig. 4-12. By controlling PC4's GUI from PC1, the compressed image received from PC2 is decompressed in PC4. The decompressed image is recognized by using the method specified in the network. Then the recognition result is sent back to PC1. The PC4's GUI is shown in Fig. 4-13. In case of multi-stage image compression, the compressed image with Compression Index (CI) is received from PC2. PC4 will decompress the received image and store it, the appropriate GUI for PC4 in case of multi-stage image compression is shown in Fig. 4-14.

The same is happened for PC5 except that there is no decompression process is performed in PC5. The GUI in PC5 is shown in Fig. 4-15. The transmission time is computed for all network PCS. The recognition time and network transmission time for Line 1 and Line 2 are compared for the methods of iris recognition as shown in Table 4-3.

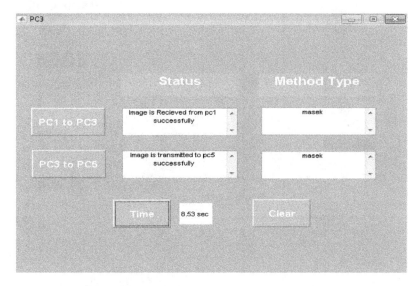

Figure 4-12 PC3's GUI.

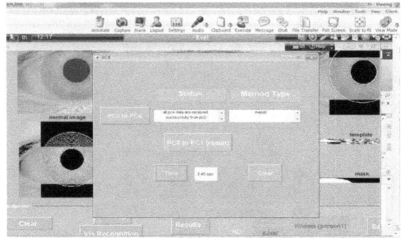

Figure 4-13 PC4's GUI.

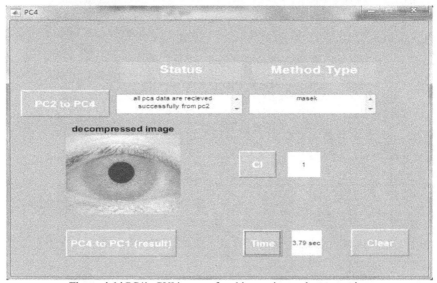

Figure 4-14 PC4's GUI in case of multi-stage image decompression.

61

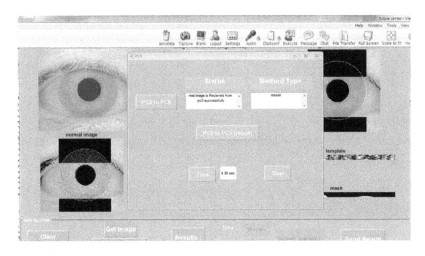

Figure 4-15 PC5's GUI.

Table 4-3: Average timing results per 25 testing samples of CASIA database.

Method name	Average transmission time (sec)		Average recognition time (sec)		Average total time (sec)	
	Line 1	Line 2	Line 1	Line 2	Line 1	Line2
Libor Masek algorithm	24.6	25.5	135.7	11.5	80.15	18.5
Genetic algorithm	23.3	24.6	9.3	6.5	16.3	15.55

The timing results in table 4-3 shows that genetic algorithm takes less execution time than Libor Masek algorithm. The recognition time of the decompressed image in Line 1 is higher than recognition time of the uncompressed image in Line 2. Line 1 transmission time is less than Line 1 because of transmitting compressed image unlike Line 2, which transmits uncompressed real image. The total time of Line 1 is higher than Line 2 for both used methods (see Appendix C).

Chapter Five

Conclusions and Suggestions for Future Work

5.1 Conclusions

During the implementation of the case studies, a number of conclusions have been drawn based on the practical results obtained from the implemented system and the following are the most important ones:

- It has been proven that genetic algorithm is more accurate than Libor Masek algorithm.
- The recognition rate of Libor Masek and genetic algorithms decreases when more samples were taken.
- It has been proven that genetic algorithm is faster than Libor Masek algorithm in recognizing iris patterns.
- PCA compression algorithm has been proven that it is the suitable for reducing iris images size while maintaining their good quality.
- Decompressed images have low compression ratios and high PSNRs ,which makes decompressed images almost the same as original images
- Multi-Stage image compression is more secure than one-stage image compression.
- It has been proven that both methods of iris pattern recognition were able to recognize reconstructed or recovered iris images.
- It has been proven that compression/decompression process of the iris images makes iris recognition process takes longer time compared with uncompressed iris images.
- Compressed images transmits faster than uncompressed images.

63

5.2 Suggestions for Future Work

To develop the present implemented work, the following suggestions are put forward:

- Adding high resolution iris camera to the proposed system to capture eye images from different kinds of individuals
- Try texture analysis method for iris pattern recognition to compare with.
- Wireless network transmission can be improved by using another backup router and set up the network as mesh topology incase if one router fail down, the network transmission will not be affected.
- Using hybrid pattern recognition.

References

[1] Jafar M. H. Ali, Aboul Ella Hassanien, "An Iris Recognition System to Enhance E-security Environment Based on Wavelet Theory", Advanced Modeling and Optimization, Vol. 5, No. 2, Kuwait, 2003.

[2] Usham Dias, Vinita Frietas, Sandeep P.S., and Amanda Fernandes, "A Neural Network Based Iris Recognition System for Personal Identification", Ictact Journal on Soft Computing, Issue: 02, India, October 2010.

[3] Gurveen K.Sandhu, Gurpreet Singh Mann, and Rajdeep Kaur, "Benefit and security issues in wireless technologies: Wi-fi and WiMax", International Journal of Innovative Research in Computer and Communication Engineering, Vol. 1, Issue 4, India, June 2013.

[4] K. Horvath, H. St¨ogner, G. Weinhandel, and A. Uhl, "Experimental Study on Lossless Compression of Biometric Iris Data", Compression Technologies and Data Formats, Austria, 2010.

[5] Mahdi S. Hosseini, Babak N. Araabi, and Hamid Soltanian-Zadeh, "Pigment Melanin: Pattern for Iris Recognition", Iran, 29 November, 2009.

[6] Lin Zhonghua, Lu Bibo, "Iris Recognition Method Based on the Coefficients of Morlet Wavelet Transform", 2010 International Conference on Intelligent Computation Technology and Automation, No.10926075, China, 2010.

[7] Eun-suk Cho, Ronnie D. Caytiles, and Seok-soo Kim, "New Algorithm Biometric-Based Iris Pattern Recognition System: Basis of Identity Authentication and Verification", Journal of Security Engineering, October 31, 2011.

[8] R. P. Ramkumar, Dr. S. Arumugam, "A Novel Iris Recognition Algorithm", ICCCNT'12, Coimbatore, India, July 2012.

[9] Samarth S. Mabrukar, Nitin S. Sonawane, and Jasmine A. Bagban, "Biometric System using Iris Pattern Recognition", International Journal of Innovative Technology and Exploring Engineering, Vol. 2, Issue-5, India, April 2013.

[10] Khalid A. Darabkh, Raed T. Al-Zubi, and Mariam T. Jaludi, "New Recognition Methods for Human Iris Patterns", MIPRO 2014, Opatija, Croatia, 26-30 May 2014.

[11] Ali Azimi Kashani, Alimohamad Monjezi Nori, and Iman Mosavian, "New methods of verification and identification using iris patterns", Journal of Scientific Research and Development, Iran, 2015.

[12] Saikat Maitra, Jun Yan, "Principle Component Analysis and Partial Least Squares: Two Dimension Reduction Techniques for Regression", Casualty Actuarial Society, 2008.

[13] Sherin Kishk, Hosam Eldin Mahmoud Ahmed, and Hala Helmy, "Integral Images Compression using Discrete Wavelets and PCA", International Journal of Signal Processing, Image Processing and Pattern Recognition, Vol. 4, No. 2, June, 2011.

[14] Rafael do Espírito Santo, "Principal Component Analysis applied to digital image compression", Brazil, June 13, 2012.

[15] Sasan Karamizadeh, Shahidan M. Abdullah, Azizah A. Manaf, Mazdak Zamani, and Alireza Hooman, "An Overview of Principal Component Analysis", Journal of Signal and Information Processing, Malaysia, 2013.

[16] Seifedine Kadry, Khaled Smaili, "A Design and Implementation of A Wireless Iris Recognition Attendance Management System", Information Technology and Control, Vol. 36, No. 3, 2007.

[17] Smita S. Mudholkar, Pradnya M. Shende, and Milind V. Sarode, "Biometrics Authentication Technique for Intrusion Detection Systems Using Fingerprint

Recognition", International Journal of Computer Science, Engineering and Information Technology, Vol.2, No.1, India, February 2012.

[18] Tatyana Dembinsky, "Measurement of the information for identification in iris images", Canada, 2006.

[19] Shivani, Er. Pooja kaushik, and Er. Yuvraj Sharma, "Design of Iris Recognition System Using Reverse Biorthogonal Wavelet for UBIRIS Database", International Journal of Scientific Research Engineering & Technology, Vol. 3, Issue 2, India, May 2014.

[20] Yong Zhu, Tieniu Tan, and Yunhong Wang, "Biometric Personal Identification Based on Iris Patterns", Chinese Academy of Sciences, China.

[21] D. de Martin- Roche, C. Sanchez-Avilat, and R. Sanchez-Reillot, "Iris Recognition for Biometric Identification using Dyadic Wavelet Transform Zero-Crossing", IEEE, Spain, 2001.

[22] Shideh Homayon, "Iris Recognition for Personal Identification Using Lamstar Neural Network", International Journal of Computer Science & Information Technology, Vol. 7, No. 1, USA, February 2015.

[23] Dr.Sudeep D. Thepade, Pooja V. Bidwai, "Contemplation of Image Based Iris Recognition", International Journal of Engineering Research and Applications, Vol. 3, Issue 2, India, March -April 2013.

[24] Libor Masek, "Recognition of Human Iris Patterns for Biometric Identification", Australia, 2003.

[25] Raziyeh Moradi, Hamid Dehghani, Ali Reza Malahzadeh, and Ali Rafiee, "Representation a New Filter to Improve Iris Segmentation in Identity Recognition Systems", IEEE, Iran, 2011.

[26] Kirti Gupta, Rashmi Gupta, "Iris Recognition System for Smart Environments", IEEE, India, 2014.

[27] Sudha Gupta, Asst. Professor, LMIETE, LMISTE, Viral Doshi, Abhinav Jain and Sreeram Iyer, "Iris Recognition System using Biometric Template Matching Technology", International Journal of Computer Applications, Vol. 1, No. 2, India, 2010.

[28] Qichuan Tian, Hua Qu, Lanfang Zhang, and Ruishan Zong, "Personal Identity Recognition Approach Based on Iris Pattern", State of the Art in Biometrics, No.65, China, July, 2011.

[29] Hasimah, and Momoh J. E. Salami, "Iris Recognition System Using Support Vector Machines", Biometric Systems, Design and Applications, No.65, Malaysia, October, 2011.

[30] Ban Ahmed Mitras, and Ammar Saad Abdul-Jabbar, "Novel Hybrid Genetic Algorithm with HMM Based Iris Recognition", International Journal of Information Technology and Business Management, Vol.15, No.1, Iraq, July 2013.

[31] Jenna Carr, "An Introduction to Genetic Algorithms", May 30, 2014.

[32] Christian Johansson, and Gustav Evertsson, "Optimizing Genetic Algorithms for Time Critical Problems", Sweden, June 2003.

[33] Kumara Sastry, David Goldberg, and Graham Kendall, "Genetic Algorithms", USA, UK.

[34] Philipp Koehn, "Combining Genetic Algorithms and Neural Networks: The Encoding Problem", Knoxville, December 1994.

[35] C. R. Prashanth, Shashikumar D.R., K. B. Raja, K. R. Venugopal, and L. M. Patnaik," High Security Human Recognition System using Iris Images", International Journal of Recent Trends in Engineering, Vol. 1, No. 1, India, May 2009.

[36]   Wei-Yu Han, Wei-Kuei Chen, Yen-Po Lee, Kuang-shyr Wu, and Jen-Chun Lee, "Iris Recognition based on Local Mean Decomposition", An International Journal of Applied Mathematics & Information Sciences, No. 1L, Taiwan, April, 2014.

[37]   Rakhi Seth, and Sanjivani Shantaiya, "A Survey on Image Compression Methods with PCA & LDA", International Journal of Science and Research, Vol. 4 Issue 4, India, April 2015.

[38]   Wei-Yi Wei, "An Introduction to Image Compression", Taiwan.

[39]   Ashutosh Dwivedi, Arvind Tolambiya, Prabhanjan Kandula, N Subhash Chandra Bose, Ashiwani Kumar, and Prem K Kalra, "Color Image Compression Using 2-Dimensional Principal Component Analysis (2DPCA)", India.

[40]   M. Mudrov´a, A. Proch´azka, "Principal Component Analysis in Image Processing", Prague.

[41]   Gurpreet Kaur, and Kamaljeet Kaur, "Image Compression using DWT and Principal Component Analysis", IOSR Journal of Electrical and Electronics Engineering, Vol. 10, Issue 3 Ver. I, May – Jun. 2015.

[42]   Aleš Hladnik, "Image Compression and Face Recognition: Two Image Processing Applications of Principal Component Analysis", International Circular of Graphic Education and Research, No. 6, 2013.

[43]   R. C. Gonzalez and R.E. Woods, "Digital Image Processing", 3rd Ed., 2008.

[44]   Arcangelo Bruna, "Principles of Image Compression", Catania, 2008.

[45]   Ian Dangerfield, and B.A, "Wireless Network Measurement: VoIP and 802.11e", Ireland, December 2007.

[46]   Matthew Gast, "802.11 Wireless Networks the Definitive Guide", USA, 2005.

[47]   Behrouz A. Forouzan, "Data Communication and Networking", Fourth Edition, New York, 2007.

[48] Shihyu Chang, "Generating Function Analysis of Wireless Networks and ARQ Systems", Michigan, 2006.

[49] "Lantronix Xport Standard Ethernet", 2013.

[50] "TCP/IP Desktop Interface RIS-0583-400", Switzerland, 2013.

[51] Alisha Cecil, "A Summary of Network Traffic Monitoring and Analysis Techniques".

[52] Ahmed Kijazi, Kisangiri Michael, "A Step on Developing Network Monitoring Tools", Computer Engineering and Intelligent Systems, Vol.5, No.8, Tanzania, 2014.

[53] M. Uma, G. Padmavathi, "An Efficient Network Traffic Monitoring for Wireless Networks", International Journal of Computer Applications, Vol. 53–No.9, September 2012.

[54] "http://www.netsupportschool.com/index.asp", United Kingdom.

[55] "http://biometrics.idealtest.org/dbDetailForUser.do?id=1", China.

[56] Aly I. Desoky, Hesham A. Ali, and Nahla B. Abdel-Hamid, "Enhancing iris recognition system performance using templates fusion", Egypt, 2011.

Published Paper:

"Design and Implementation of Iris Pattern Recognition using Wireless Network System", Journal of Computer and Communications, Volume 4, No.7, May 2016.

Appendix A – Iris Recognition Results

Table A-1 Recognition results for Libor Masek algorithm.

Person no.	Test image no.1	Test image no.2	Test image no.3
1	Matched	Matched	Matched
2	Matched	Matched	Matched
3	Matched	Matched	Matched
4	Matched	Matched	Matched
5	Matched	Matched	Matched
6	Matched	Matched	Matched
7	Matched	Matched	Matched
8	Matched	Matched	Matched
9	Matched	Matched	Matched
10	Matched	Matched	Matched
11	Matched	Matched	Matched
12	Matched	Matched	Matched
13	Matched	Matched	Matched
14	Matched	Matched	Matched
15	Matched	Matched	Matched
16	Matched	Matched	Matched
17	Matched	Matched	Matched
18	Matched	Matched	Not Matched
19	Matched	Matched	Matched
20	Matched	Matched	Matched
21	Matched	Matched	Matched
22	Matched	Matched	Matched
23	Matched	Matched	Matched
24	Matched	Matched	Matched
25	Matched	Matched	Matched
26	Matched	Matched	Matched
27	Matched	Matched	Matched
28	Matched	Matched	Matched
29	Matched	Matched	Matched
30	Matched	Matched	Matched
31	Matched	Matched	Matched
32	Matched	Matched	Matched
33	Matched	Matched	Matched
34	Matched	Matched	Matched
35	Matched	Matched	Matched
36	Matched	Matched	Matched
37	Matched	Matched	Matched

38	Matched	Matched	Matched
39	Matched	Matched	Matched
40	Matched	Matched	Matched
41	Matched	Matched	Matched
42	Matched	Matched	Matched
43	Matched	Matched	Matched
44	Matched	Matched	Matched
45	Matched	Matched	Matched
46	Not Matched	Matched	Matched
47	Matched	Matched	Matched
48	Matched	Matched	Matched
49	Matched	Matched	Matched
50	Matched	Matched	Matched
51	Matched	Matched	Matched
52	Not Matched	Matched	Matched
53	Matched	Matched	Matched
54	Matched	Matched	Matched
55	Matched	Matched	Matched
56	Matched	Matched	Matched
57	Matched	Matched	Matched
58	Not Matched	Not Matched	Matched
59	Matched	Matched	Matched
60	Matched	Matched	Matched
61	Matched	Matched	Matched
62	Matched	Matched	Matched
63	Matched	Matched	Matched
64	Matched	Matched	Matched
65	Matched	Matched	Matched
66	Not Matched	Matched	Matched
67	Matched	Matched	Matched
68	Matched	Matched	Matched
69	Matched	Matched	Matched
70	Matched	Not Matched	Matched
71	Matched	Matched	Matched
72	Matched	Matched	Matched
73	Not Matched	Matched	Matched
74	Matched	Matched	Matched
75	Matched	Matched	Matched
76	Matched	Matched	Matched
77	Matched	Matched	Matched
78	Matched	Matched	Matched
79	Matched	Matched	Matched
80	Matched	Matched	Matched

B

81	Matched	Not Matched	Matched
82	Matched	Matched	Matched
83	Matched	Matched	Matched
84	Matched	Matched	Matched
85	Not Matched	Matched	Matched
86	Matched	Matched	Matched
87	Matched	Matched	Matched
88	Not Matched	Matched	Matched
89	Matched	Matched	Matched
90	Matched	Matched	Matched
91	Not Matched	Matched	Matched
92	Matched	Matched	Matched
93	Matched	Matched	Matched
94	Matched	Matched	Matched
95	Not Matched	Matched	Matched
96	Matched	Matched	Matched
97	Matched	Matched	Matched
98	Matched	Matched	Matched
99	Matched	Matched	Matched
100	Matched	Matched	Matched
101	Matched	Matched	Matched
102	Matched	Matched	Matched
103	Matched	Matched	Matched
104	Matched	Matched	Not Matched
105	Matched	Matched	Matched
106	Not Matched	Not Matched	Matched
107	Matched	Matched	Matched
108	Matched	Matched	Matched

Table A-2 Recognition results for genetic algorithm.

Person no.	Test image no.1	Test image no.2	Test image no.3
1	Matched	Matched	Matched
2	Matched	Matched	Matched
3	Matched	Matched	Matched
4	Matched	Matched	Matched
5	Matched	Matched	Matched
6	Matched	Matched	Matched
7	Matched	Matched	Matched
8	Matched	Matched	Matched
9	Matched	Matched	Matched

10	Matched	Matched	Matched
11	Matched	Matched	Matched
12	Matched	Matched	Matched
13	Matched	Matched	Matched
14	Matched	Matched	Matched
15	Matched	Matched	Matched
16	Matched	Matched	Matched
17	Matched	Matched	Matched
18	Matched	Matched	Matched
19	Matched	Matched	Matched
20	Matched	Matched	Matched
21	Matched	Matched	Matched
22	Matched	Matched	Matched
23	Matched	Matched	Matched
24	Matched	Matched	Matched
25	Matched	Matched	Matched
26	Matched	Matched	Matched
27	Matched	Matched	Matched
28	Matched	Matched	Matched
29	Matched	Matched	Matched
30	Matched	Matched	Matched
31	Matched	Matched	Matched
32	Matched	Matched	Matched
33	Matched	Matched	Matched
34	Matched	Matched	Matched
35	Matched	Matched	Matched
36	Matched	Matched	Matched
37	Matched	Matched	Matched
38	Matched	Matched	Matched
39	Matched	Matched	Matched
40	Matched	Matched	Matched
41	Matched	Matched	Matched
42	Matched	Matched	Matched
43	Matched	Matched	Matched
44	Matched	Matched	Matched
45	Matched	Matched	Matched
46	False Matched	Matched	Matched
47	Matched	Matched	Matched
48	Matched	Matched	Matched
49	Matched	Matched	Matched
50	Matched	Matched	Matched
51	Matched	Matched	Matched
52	Matched	Matched	Matched

D

53	Matched	Matched	Matched
54	Matched	Matched	Matched
55	Matched	Matched	Matched
56	Matched	Matched	Matched
57	Matched	Matched	Matched
58	False Matched	False Matched	Matched
59	Matched	Matched	Matched
60	Matched	Matched	Matched
61	Matched	Matched	Matched
62	Matched	Matched	Matched
63	Matched	Matched	Matched
64	Matched	Matched	Matched
65	Matched	Matched	Matched
66	Matched	Matched	Matched
67	False Matched	Matched	Matched
68	Matched	Matched	Matched
69	Matched	Matched	Matched
70	Matched	Matched	Matched
71	Matched	Matched	Matched
72	Matched	Matched	Matched
73	False Matched	Matched	Matched
74	Matched	Matched	Matched
75	Matched	Matched	Matched
76	Matched	Matched	Matched
77	Matched	Matched	Matched
78	Matched	Matched	Matched
79	Matched	Matched	Matched
80	Matched	Matched	Matched
81	Matched	False Matched	Matched
82	Matched	Matched	Matched
83	Matched	Matched	Matched
84	Matched	Matched	Matched
85	Matched	Matched	Matched
86	Matched	Matched	Matched
87	Matched	Matched	Matched
88	Matched	Matched	Matched
89	Matched	Matched	Matched
90	Matched	Matched	Matched
91	Matched	Matched	Matched
92	Matched	Matched	Matched
93	Matched	Matched	Matched
94	Matched	Matched	Matched
95	Matched	Matched	Matched

E

96	Matched	Matched	Matched
97	Matched	Matched	Matched
98	Matched	Matched	Matched
99	Matched	Matched	Matched
100	Matched	Matched	Matched
101	Matched	Matched	Matched
102	Matched	Matched	Matched
103	Matched	Matched	Matched
104	Matched	Matched	False Matched
105	Matched	Matched	Matched
106	False Matched	False Matched	Matched
107	Matched	Matched	Matched
108	Matched	Matched	Matched

Appendix B – Quality Measurements of Decompressed Iris Image

Table B-1 Compression Ratios for 75 samples.

Person no.	Test image no.1	Test image no.2	Test image no.3	Average CR
1	3.23	3.12	3.12	3.15
2	3.17	3.20	3.13	3.16
3	3.3	3.3	3.23	3.27
4	3.24	3.2	3.2	3.21
5	3.16	3.27	3.16	3.19
6	3.20	3.17	3.2	3.19
7	3.31	3.2	3.31	3.27
8	3.24	3.06	3.17	3.15
9	3.10	3.06	3.13	3.09
10	3.1	3.13	3.06	3.09
11	3.24	3.2	3.24	3.22
12	3.23	3.16	3.27	3.22
13	3.10	3.17	3.13	3.13
14	3.13	3.20	3.1	3.14
15	3.09	3.19	3.16	3.14
16	3.34	3.27	3.27	3.29
17	3.42	3.27	3.20	3.29
18	3.17	3.1	3.17	3.14
19	3.23	3.2	3.26	3.23

20	3.03	3.03	3.07	3.04
21	3.16	3.16	3.26	3.19
22	3.16	3.09	3.2	3.15
23	3.2	3.33	3.3	3.27
24	3.31	3.2	3.2	3.23
25	3.13	3.24	3.16	3.17

Table B-2 PSNRs for 75 samples.

Person no.	Test image no.1	Test image no.2	Test image no.3	Average PSNR
1	300.01	300.28	299.76	300.68
2	301.49	301.19	300.97	301.21
3	300.50	298.19	300.22	299.63
4	299.43	297.75	299.30	298.82
5	300.04	300.54	300.77	300.45
6	301.29	300.37	301.97	301.21
7	299.57	300.14	299.49	299.73
8	300.21	299.30	298.76	299.42
9	300.77	299.72	300.89	300.46
10	298.30	299.57	298.38	298.75
11	299.77	300.22	299.66	299.88
12	300.32	300.28	299.53	300.04
13	301.34	301.50	301.58	301.47
14	299.24	300.93	301.15	300.44
15	301.35	301.74	300.08	301.05
16	301.01	300.38	300.64	300.67
17	301.14	302.02	298.72	300.62
18	301.53	301.72	298.16	300.47
19	299.29	299.43	299.56	299.42
20	299.34	299.03	298.93	299.1
21	298.97	300.75	300.65	300.12
22	300.90	300.15	300.98	300.67
23	297.89	298.91	298.73	298.51
24	299.62	298.54	301.56	299.90
25	300.95	300.90	300.31	300.72

G

Appendix C – Timing Results

Table C-1 Timing results for Libor Masek algorithm.

Image no.	PC to PC	Transmission time (sec)	Recognition time (sec)	
			Decompressed image	Real image
001-1-2	PC1 to PC2	14.89	134.16	10.66
	PC1 to PC3	13.88		
	PC2 to PC4	11.35		
	PC3 to PC5	12.83		
	PC4 to PC1	4.14		
	PC5 to PC1	4.45		
002-1-2	PC1 to PC2	13.02	141.05	12.01
	PC1 to PC3	12.91		
	PC2 to PC4	12.27		
	PC3 to PC5	13.17		
	PC4 to PC1	3.81		
	PC5 to PC1	4.81		
003-1-2	PC1 to PC2	9.21	180.04	14.80
	PC1 to PC3	10.43		
	PC2 to PC4	10.66		
	PC3 to PC5	14.60		
	PC4 to PC1	4.16		
	PC5 to PC1	5.25		
004-1-2	PC1 to PC2	7.93	109.56	9.40
	PC1 to PC3	9.01		
	PC2 to PC4	10.41		
	PC3 to PC5	11.18		
	PC4 to PC1	4.77		
	PC5 to PC1	4.10		
005-1-2	PC1 to PC2	14.59	114.88	9.54
	PC1 to PC3	14.65		
	PC2 to PC4	14.20		
	PC3 to PC5	17.46		
	PC4 to PC1	3.58		
	PC5 to PC1	3.24		
006-1-2	PC1 to PC2	10.85	115.77	9.79
	PC1 to PC3	9.75		
	PC2 to PC4	9.73		
	PC3 to PC5	7.43		
	PC4 to PC1	3.00		
	PC5 to PC1	3.57		

H

007-1-2	PC1 to PC2	8.61	137.67	11.61
	PC1 to PC3	12.28		
	PC2 to PC4	5.34		
	PC3 to PC5	10.01		
	PC4 to PC1	3.52		
	PC5 to PC1	3.50		
008-1-3	PC1 to PC2	8.18	112.63	9.65
	PC1 to PC3	12.45		
	PC2 to PC4	6.60		
	PC3 to PC5	9.32		
	PC4 to PC1	3.71		
	PC5 to PC1	5.25		
009-1-2	PC1 to PC2	7.22	78.93	6.72
	PC1 to PC3	8.59		
	PC2 to PC4	9.09		
	PC3 to PC5	9.39		
	PC4 to PC1	4.52		
	PC5 to PC1	4.02		
010-1-2	PC1 to PC2	7.81	188.80	15.35
	PC1 to PC3	7.98		
	PC2 to PC4	10.81		
	PC3 to PC5	10.22		
	PC4 to PC1	3.67		
	PC5 to PC1	3.34		
011-1-2	PC1 to PC2	7.96	109.10	8.80
	PC1 to PC3	7.12		
	PC2 to PC4	5.32		
	PC3 to PC5	5.39		
	PC4 to PC1	5.04		
	PC5 to PC1	3.44		
012-1-2	PC1 to PC2	6.87	127.96	10.50
	PC1 to PC3	8.62		
	PC2 to PC4	9.42		
	PC3 to PC5	9.48		
	PC4 to PC1	3.65		
	PC5 to PC1	4.06		
013-1-2	PC1 to PC2	7.21	105.59	8.68
	PC1 to PC3	8.52		
	PC2 to PC4	9.51		
	PC3 to PC5	11.40		
	PC4 to PC1	3.38		
	PC5 to PC1	4.43		
	PC1 to PC2	9.40		
	PC1 to PC3	9.37		

014-1-2	PC2 to PC4	8.29	136.79	11.20
	PC3 to PC5	6.89		
	PC4 to PC1	3.58		
	PC5 to PC1	3.35		
015-2-4	PC1 to PC2	6.50	187.91	16.54
	PC1 to PC3	6.86		
	PC2 to PC4	10.90		
	PC3 to PC5	10.48		
	PC4 to PC1	4.07		
	PC5 to PC1	4.44		
016-1-2	PC1 to PC2	9.53	121.73	10.67
	PC1 to PC3	7.17		
	PC2 to PC4	6.74		
	PC3 to PC5	6.99		
	PC4 to PC1	4.21		
	PC5 to PC1	3.57		
017-1-2	PC1 to PC2	8.08	124.09	10.95
	PC1 to PC3	8.62		
	PC2 to PC4	13.26		
	PC3 to PC5	14.97		
	PC4 to PC1	4.14		
	PC5 to PC1	4.62		
018-1-1	PC1 to PC2	10.89	82.70	7.54
	PC1 to PC3	8.09		
	PC2 to PC4	5.84		
	PC3 to PC5	5.95		
	PC4 to PC1	4.05		
	PC5 to PC1	3.56		
019-1-3	PC1 to PC2	8.56	206.80	17.57
	PC1 to PC3	8.75		
	PC2 to PC4	7.02		
	PC3 to PC5	11.05		
	PC4 to PC1	3.72		
	PC5 to PC1	3.77		
020-1-2	PC1 to PC2	7.49	101.07	8.99
	PC1 to PC3	6.58		
	PC2 to PC4	12.26		
	PC3 to PC5	12.62		
	PC4 to PC1	4.23		
	PC5 to PC1	3.78		
021-1-3	PC1 to PC2	6.68	146.37	12.42
	PC1 to PC3	8.51		
	PC2 to PC4	11.21		
	PC3 to PC5	9.39		

J

Image no.	PC to PC	Transmission time (sec)	Recognition time (sec)	
			Decompressed image	Real image
	PC4 to PC1	3.51		
	PC5 to PC1	3.66		
022-1-2	PC1 to PC2	12.38	168.18	14.64
	PC1 to PC3	12.30		
	PC2 to PC4	9.43		
	PC3 to PC5	9.76		
	PC4 to PC1	3.81		
	PC5 to PC1	3.24		
023-1-2	PC1 to PC2	9.74	162.66	14.00
	PC1 to PC3	7.33		
	PC2 to PC4	7.44		
	PC3 to PC5	6.35		
	PC4 to PC1	3.73		
	PC5 to PC1	3.46		
024-1-2	PC1 to PC2	15.80	127.35	10.99
	PC1 to PC3	7.47		
	PC2 to PC4	6.79		
	PC3 to PC5	6.88		
	PC4 to PC1	3.27		
	PC5 to PC1	3.65		
025-1-3	PC1 to PC2	7.68	171.50	14.76
	PC1 to PC3	7.92		
	PC2 to PC4	11.31		
	PC3 to PC5	11.05		
	PC4 to PC1	3.33		
	PC5 to PC1	4.86		

Table C-2 Timing results for genetic algorithm.

Image no.	PC to PC	Transmission time (sec)	Recognition time (sec)	
			Decompressed image	Real image
001-1-2	PC1 to PC2	8.42	10.06	5.094
	PC1 to PC3	8.81		
	PC2 to PC4	9.16		
	PC3 to PC5	9.94		
	PC4 to PC1	3.94		
	PC5 to PC1	3.88		
002-1-2	PC1 to PC2	9.76	10.64	7.02
	PC1 to PC3	9.58		
	PC2 to PC4	9.68		
	PC3 to PC5	9.73		

K

	PC4 to PC1	3.58		
	PC5 to PC1	4.84		
003-1-2	PC1 to PC2	9.82	15.04	8.91
	PC1 to PC3	9.27		
	PC2 to PC4	13.13		
	PC3 to PC5	13.14		
	PC4 to PC1	4.23		
	PC5 to PC1	4.33		
004-1-2	PC1 to PC2	7.09	8.10	5.15
	PC1 to PC3	10.88		
	PC2 to PC4	8.14		
	PC3 to PC5	12.70		
	PC4 to PC1	3.56		
	PC5 to PC1	3.40		
005-1-2	PC1 to PC2	8.26	8.40	5.65
	PC1 to PC3	8.80		
	PC2 to PC4	8.04		
	PC3 to PC5	11.79		
	PC4 to PC1	3.54		
	PC5 to PC1	3.13		
006-1-2	PC1 to PC2	6.50	8.66	5.74
	PC1 to PC3	6.92		
	PC2 to PC4	7.67		
	PC3 to PC5	8.40		
	PC4 to PC1	3.52		
	PC5 to PC1	3.35		
007-1-2	PC1 to PC2	8.25	9.87	6.88
	PC1 to PC3	8.47		
	PC2 to PC4	8.50		
	PC3 to PC5	11.32		
	PC4 to PC1	6.76		
	PC5 to PC1	5.01		
008-1-3	PC1 to PC2	10.71	7.92	5.64
	PC1 to PC3	10.63		
	PC2 to PC4	7.28		
	PC3 to PC5	16.59		
	PC4 to PC1	4.51		
	PC5 to PC1	4.54		
009-1-2	PC1 to PC2	10.99	5.53	3.59
	PC1 to PC3	14.27		
	PC2 to PC4	10.85		
	PC3 to PC5	11.67		
	PC4 to PC1	4.60		
	PC5 to PC1	3.55		

L

010-1-2	PC1 to PC2	16.59	15.77	9.56
	PC1 to PC3	11.33		
	PC2 to PC4	8.24		
	PC3 to PC5	9.68		
	PC4 to PC1	4.85		
	PC5 to PC1	4.67		
011-1-2	PC1 to PC2	11.66	7.53	5.11
	PC1 to PC3	12.56		
	PC2 to PC4	7.83		
	PC3 to PC5	11.51		
	PC4 to PC1	3.37		
	PC5 to PC1	3.69		
012-1-2	PC1 to PC2	6.30	9.09	5.57
	PC1 to PC3	6.06		
	PC2 to PC4	9.19		
	PC3 to PC5	12.63		
	PC4 to PC1	3.22		
	PC5 to PC1	3.80		
013-1-2	PC1 to PC2	6.47	7.87	5.10
	PC1 to PC3	7.69		
	PC2 to PC4	8.93		
	PC3 to PC5	8.99		
	PC4 to PC1	4.31		
	PC5 to PC1	3.68		
014-1-2	PC1 to PC2	10.40	7.30	5.77
	PC1 to PC3	7.53		
	PC2 to PC4	9.38		
	PC3 to PC5	10.20		
	PC4 to PC1	3.79		
	PC5 to PC1	3.27		
015-2-4	PC1 to PC2	6.47	13.69	9.40
	PC1 to PC3	6.40		
	PC2 to PC4	9.65		
	PC3 to PC5	10.73		
	PC4 to PC1	3.28		
	PC5 to PC1	5.82		
016-1-2	PC1 to PC2	13.68	10.62	5.81
	PC1 to PC3	7.12		
	PC2 to PC4	7.33		
	PC3 to PC5	8.54		
	PC4 to PC1	3.56		
	PC5 to PC1	3.99		
	PC1 to PC2	10.21		
	PC1 to PC3	13.82		

M

017-1-2	PC2 to PC4	8.22	9.01	6.16
	PC3 to PC5	7.62		
	PC4 to PC1	3.16		
	PC5 to PC1	3.28		
018-1-1	PC1 to PC2	7.03	3.98	3.93
	PC1 to PC3	7.39		
	PC2 to PC4	7.66		
	PC3 to PC5	9.14		
	PC4 to PC1	3.34		
	PC5 to PC1	3.30		
019-1-3	PC1 to PC2	8.85	15.13	10.47
	PC1 to PC3	6.79		
	PC2 to PC4	8.25		
	PC3 to PC5	8.83		
	PC4 to PC1	3.49		
	PC5 to PC1	5.09		
020-1-2	PC1 to PC2	6.94	4.80	4.72
	PC1 to PC3	6.97		
	PC2 to PC4	10.01		
	PC3 to PC5	15.65		
	PC4 to PC1	4.10		
	PC5 to PC1	3.62		
021-1-3	PC1 to PC2	6.59	7.44	6.39
	PC1 to PC3	6.68		
	PC2 to PC4	5.92		
	PC3 to PC5	8.40		
	PC4 to PC1	3.45		
	PC5 to PC1	4.33		
022-1-2	PC1 to PC2	7.79	12.57	8.47
	PC1 to PC3	6.43		
	PC2 to PC4	12.38		
	PC3 to PC5	11.23		
	PC4 to PC1	5.12		
	PC5 to PC1	3.40		
023-1-2	PC1 to PC2	9.00	8.07	7.98
	PC1 to PC3	10.16		
	PC2 to PC4	11.94		
	PC3 to PC5	9.75		
	PC4 to PC1	4.34		
	PC5 to PC1	3.63		
024-1-2	PC1 to PC2	8.51	6.63	6.62
	PC1 to PC3	6.53		
	PC2 to PC4	9.24		
	PC3 to PC5	8.40		

N

	PC4 to PC1	5.21		
	PC5 to PC1	4.75		
025-1-3	PC1 to PC2	9.08	9.12	7.78
	PC1 to PC3	7.49		
	PC2 to PC4	8.60		
	PC3 to PC5	8.69		
	PC4 to PC1	3.82		
	PC5 to PC1	4.53		

O

الخلاصه

الهدف من هذه الرسالة هو اقتراح نظام التعرف على نمط قزحية العين سريع ودقيق باستخدام نظام شبكة لاسلكية. العمل في هذه الأطروحة يقسم الى ثلاثة أجزاء. يتضمن الجزء الأول، خوارزمية Libor Masek المعدله لتحقيق أعلى نسبة تمييز للانماط. وتم استخدام طريقة أخرى للتعرف على نمط قزحية الذي يدعى الخوارزمية الجينية. وتم مقارنة الطريقتين للتعرف على قزحية العين وفقا للدقة و للزمن المستغرق في التنفيذ. عند اجراء الاختبار المأخوذه من الأكاديمية الصينية للعلوم في معهد قاعدة بيانات الأتمتة (CASIA) ، حققت كلتا الطريقتين نسبة بدقه بلغت 100 ٪ لتمييز الانماط أذ تتطابق صوره واحده على الاقل من ثلاث صور لكل شخص. ولكن عند اجراء الاختبار لكل صوره من الصورة ولكل الأشخاص باستخدام قاعدة(CASIA) ، حققت الخوارزمية الجينية أعلى معدلات الدقه في تمييز الانماط و بالمقابل ادنى معدلات الخطأ مقارنه مع من خوارزمية Libor Masek و أن زمن التنفيذ المستغرق في تمييز الانماط من قبل الخوارزمية الجينية أقل من خوارزمية Libor Masek. فيما يتضمن الجزء الثاني، ضغط واعادة فتح صورة قزحية العين المضغوطه باستخدام تحليل المكونات الرئيسه (PCA) لعملية الضغط ومعكوس تحليل المكونات الرئيسه (IPCA) لعملية إزالة الضغط. وقد ثبت أن PCA هو الأسلوب الأنسب لضغط قزحية الصور بسبب قدرته على تقليل حجمها مع الحفاظ على نوعية جيدة من الصور. والصور التي أعيد فتحها باستخدام IPCA لها نسب منخفضة الضغط (CRS)وقيمة عالية لنسب الإشارة(PSNRs). لحمايه اكثر، طبقت عمليه ضغط الصوره لعده مرات لغرض حمايه عمليه ارسال معلومات الشبكات من الهكرز، لان الهكرز لايمكن ان يحزر كم عدد المرات التي ضغطت بها الصوره.

واخيرا يتضمن الجزء الثالث، تصميم وبناء نظام شبكة لاسلكية تتكون من كمبيوتر شخصي مركزي (PC)، وأربعة أجهزة الكمبيوتر الشخصية (أجهزة الكمبيوتر) التي تتصل مع بعضها البعض من خلال جهاز التوجيه. يأخذ جهاز الكمبيوتر المركزي مسؤولية مراقبة والسيطرة على أجهزة الكمبيوتر على الشبكة بأكملها. يتم التواصل مع جميع أجهزة الشبكة بعضها مع البعض باستخدام بروتوكول التحكم بالإرسال / بروتوكول الإنترنت(TCP /IP) . من النتائج التي تم الحصول عليها، كانت الخوارزمية الجينية اسرع في تمييز صورة القزحية التي أعيد فتح الضغط عنها في مدة أقل من خوارزمية Libor Masek. يستغرق الخط الأول وقت اقل مقارنه مع الخط الثاني.

شُكر وتَقدير

بعد أن تم بفضل الله سبحانه وتعالى إنجاز مشروعي هذا، أتقدم بجزيل الشكر والتقدير الى الاستاذ الفاضل الدكتور المشرف علي عبد الحافظ ابراهيم لما أبداه من توجيهات وإشراف. كما يسعدني أن أشكر عميد كلية هندسة المعلومات وجميع أساتذتي الأفاضل على دعمهم المتواصل أثناء فترة الدراسة وشكري العميق الى كادر كلية هندسة المعلومات والى كل من قدم لي المساعدة لإنجاز هذا المشروع.

ولا يفوتني أن أعبر عن خالص امتناني وشكري الى جميع أفراد عائلتي وبالأخص والدتي العزيزة لما قدمت لي من مساعدة وتوجيهات خلال مسيرتي الدراسية.

فألى كل أولئك أسأل الله تعالى أن يمنّ عليهم بالصحة والسلامة ويحفظهم ويوفقهم لكل خير.

ذرى علي خلف

2016

تصميم وبناء نظام التعرف على نمط قزحية العين المرتكز على نظام الشبكه اللاسلكيه

رسالة

مقدمة إلى كلية هندسة المعلومات في جامعة النهرين

كجزء من متطلبات نيل درجة ماجستير علوم

في

هندسة المعلومات والاتصالات

من قبل

ذرى علي خلف

(بكالوريوس علوم في هندسة الشبكه الدوليه 2013 م)

شوال   1437هـ

تموز   2014 م